AF369258

THE FOUNDATIONS
OF THE KARKARIYA ORDER

THE FOUNDATIONS OF THE KARKARIYA ORDER

By the Moroccan Sufi Master
SHAYKH MOHAMED FAOUZI AL-KARKARI

Translated by
Yousef CASEWIT, Khalid WILLIAMS, Jamil ZAGHDOUDI

The Foundations of the Karkariya Order is published
by the nonprofit organization Anwar
and its publishing house **Les 7 Lectures**

44, Fernand Brunfaut Street
1080 Brussels, Belgium

ISBN: 978-2-930978-56-7
Deposit number: D/2021/14.291/06 (Belgium)
Legal Deposit: September 2021

Table of Contents

أعوذ بالله من الشيطان الرجيم

بسم الله الرحمن الرحيم

بسم الله الرحمن الرحيم

بسم الله الرحمن الرحيم

بسم الله

بسم الله

بسم الله

الله

الله

الله

ولا حول ولا قوة إلا بالله العلي العظيم

Introduction

I seek refuge in God from Satan the accursed
In the Name of God, the All-Merciful, the Ever-Merciful
In the Name of God, the All-Merciful, the Ever-Merciful
In the Name of God, the All-Merciful, the Ever-Merciful
In the Name of God
In the Name of God
In the Name of God
Allāh Allāh
Allāh
There is no power nor strength but in God,
the Sublime, the Magnificent

Blessings and greetings of peace be upon the noblest
Messenger, our master Muḥammad, and upon His family,
companions, and those who follow them virtuously
until the Day of Requital

The science of Sufism is the most noble science, inasmuch as it is the spirit of our primordial religion, the quintessence and foundation of all sciences, and the highest level of religion.[1] It is thus necessary to clarify the milestones of this Path to facilitate its traversal for all those who love God and aspire to know Him. The Path is clear and manifest. The beloved ﷺ summarized it in a perfect and all-inclusive sentence: 'To worship God as if you see Him.'[2] Then God's folk came forth to clarify its milestones and explain its subtle allusions. They accomplished for Sufism what the four leading Imams [Mālik, Abū Ḥanīfa, al-Shāfiʿī, and Ibn Ḥanbal], may God have mercy on them, accomplished for jurisprudence (*fiqh*) and legal theory (*uṣūl*).

In the *Ḥikam*, it is said: "God disposed certain people for His service, and others He singled out for His love. **Each do We aid—both these and those—with the Gift of thy Lord; and the Gift of thy Lord is not confined.**"[3] As a result, disagreement arose between those who love without knowledge, and those who have zeal without deliberation. For our part, we have taken it upon ourselves to never look upon anyone who bears wit-

1   The original Arabic title of this book is *Al-Kawākib al-durriyya fī bayan al-uṣūl al-nūrāniyya*, "The Resplendent Planets: An Explanation of the Luminous Principles of the Karkariya Order" (first published in Casablanca: Maṭbaʿat Ṣināʿat al-Kitāb, 2013). The following English translation was made possible through the generous support of Abdullah Elkammar, Saif Islam, the insightful elucidations of Mohammed Amine Ghazi, as well as the editorial assistance of Fatima Casewit and Ramzi Taleb.

2   Muslim, *Ṣaḥīḥ*, K. al-Īmān, 102.

3   Q Isrāʾ 17:20. See Danner's translation of *The Book of Wisdom*, aphorism #68, p. 64.

ness to the oneness of the Real with an eye of contempt or condescension, for we are mindful of their sanctity in God's sight. Indeed, God has graced us by planting mercy for every Muslim in our hearts, and making all of His creation beloved unto us.

Furthermore, the Real has bestowed upon us knowledge from Himself. He gives to whomever He wishes through His grace and gratuitous kindness, and He deprives whomever He wishes through His justice and decree.

To this effect, Sīdī 'Abd al-Qādir b. Muḥammad (d. 1616), may God sanctify his secret, wrote:

God bestows His bounty upon whomever He wills,
Through His sheer grace, gratuitous favor, and mercy.

And whenever He elects a servant to delight in His proximity,
He chooses Him freely, and for no particular cause.

And He deprives whomever He wills, by His justice, and withholds
The overflowing of His grace, though there is no shortage of it.

This, then, is a science that we do not keep secret from His creatures. According to Abū Sa'īd al-Khudrī (d. 693), God's Messenger ﷺ said, "Whoever hides knowledge by which God benefits people in religious matters, God will bridle him on the Day of Arising with a bridle of fire."[4] We thus do not keep this

---

4   Ibn Mājah, *Sunan, Bāb man su'ila 'an 'ilm fa-katamahu,* #265, p. 97.

science secret from those who are worthy of it, just as we do not divulge it to those who are heedless of God, who mock and turn away. Likewise, we shall not transmit this science to anyone for the sake of earning their approval, exonerating ourselves from the statements and actions of the Sufis in order for so-and-so to be pleased with us. God says: **Those who convey God's messages and fear Him, and fear none but God—and God suffices as a Reckoner.**[5] We have no time to waste in delving into matters that would only lead to the resuscitation of old debates and rivalries between people who have already returned to their Lord. We only ask God to pardon them and to have mercy upon them.

Everything we pen in this book is corroborated by a holy Qur'ānic verse or a noble hadith. Therefore, if the reader finds anything that appears to be in conflict with these sacred texts, the contradiction stems not from what we intend to say, but from the reader's misunderstanding. Indeed, viewpoints may differ due to perspective, and owing to the multiple meanings that a single technical term may carry. Let us therefore excuse one another, for as one transmitted report puts it: "There are two traits that are not exceeded in goodness by any others: to presume well of God, and to presume well of God's servants.

---

5   Q Aḥzāb 33:39.

And there are two traits that are not exceeded in evil by any others: to presume ill of God, and to presume ill of God's servants."[6]

That said, we shall proceed in this book by identifying our technical terms linguistically, since language provides ample space to minimize the scope of disagreement. We shall follow by presenting, with God's permission, the meaning of the technical terms in our blessed Sufi order (*ṭarīqa*), then in the Holy Qur'ān, then in the noble hadith, then within whatever topics branch off from that.

It behooves you, dear reader, to hold fast to God's transcendence (*tanzīh*), and to forswear His immanent similarity (*tanzīh*), as He says: **Nothing is as His like, and He is the Hearing, the Seeing.**[7] You must cling to this, so that the Real may grant you insight into the realities of esoteric sciences, and enable you to imbibe from the river of gnosis. The master Muḥyī l-Dīn Ibn 'Arabī (d. 1240), may God sanctify his secret, said: "Those who hold that God dwells within His creation (*ḥulūl*) are defective in their religion, and those who hold that God becomes unified with creation (*ittiḥād*) are none other than heretics."[8]

---

6   Ibn 'Ajība cites it as a ḥadīth in *al-Baḥr al-madīd* in his commentary on Q Ḥujurāt 49:12. According Albānī, this report probably originates from Ghazālī's *Iḥyā' 'ulūm al-dīn*. See Albānī, *Silsilat al-aḥādīth al-ḍa'īfa*, vol. 1, p. 63.

7   Q Shūrā 42:11.

8   This saying by Ibn 'Arabī is not found in the *Futūḥāt*.

Beware of denying anything of this science, for those who deny the least thing are deprived of its blessing. By his nature, the human being is hostile to whatever he is ignorant of. God says: **man is the most contentious of beings.**[9]

Our approach, by God's grace, is lucid, simple and uncompounded. It is easy and smooth, and it consists of seven foundational principles:

1. The Pact (*'ahd*) along with the Rosary (*subḥa*)
2. The Sacred Dance (*al-ḥaḍra*)
3. The Patched Cloak (*al-muraqqaʿa*)
4. The Singular Name: *Allāh* (*al-ism al-mufrad*)
5. Wandering (*al-siyāḥa*)
6. The Spiritual Retreat (*khalwa*)
7. The Innermost Secret (*sirr*)

We have encapsulated these principles into an aphorism that we bequeath unto you as a guiding lantern, lest you lose your way and veer off the Shining Path (*al-maḥajja al-bayḍāʾ*).

We say:

"Abase yourself and exalt others."

That is, cling to the grounds of sheer servanthood, grounds that are devoid of the fragrance of lordship over anything in creation. Cling to the grounds of lowliness, humility, and calm repose. Make a home for your heart upon the foundation of

---

9   Q Kahf 18:54.

mercy and humility toward all of God's creatures, even if it be an insect, for it may be like the ant of our master Solomon, of which God says: **When they came to the valley of the ants, an ant said, 'O ants! Enter your dwellings, lest Solomon and his hosts crush you, while they are unaware.' And he smiled, laughing at her words, and said, 'My Lord! Inspire me to give thanks for Thy blessing wherewith Thou hast blessed me and my parents, and to work righteousness pleasing to Thee; and cause me to enter, through Thy Mercy, among Thy righteous servants!'** [10] Or even if it be toward a tree, for Moses was addressed from the tree: **And when he came upon [the side of the Mount], he was called from the right bank of the valley, at the blessed site, from the tree, 'O Moses! Approach and fear not! Truly, I am God, Lord of the worlds!'** [11] Revere all of God's creation, and pass away from your lower self and its appetites. Beware of excessive chatter, and be in the company of those who assist you in your religious affairs. Make your tongue soft with the remembrance of God, and yours shall be a state of wellbeing in the herebelow, and felicity in the Hereafter.

10   Q Naml 27:18-20.
11   Q Qaṣaṣ 28:30.

1.

The Pact (*al-ʿahd*)

In the Arabic language:

The word *ʿahd* means a covenant (*mīthāq*), oath (*yamīn*), or promise (*waʿd*).[12]

In the Terminology of the Karkariya Order:

The pact denotes a pure proclamation of divine oneness (*tawḥīd*), as expressed at the moment when the first Covenant was taken in the [pre-cosmic] World of the Seed (*ʿālam al-dharr*) with the children of Adam, and wherein lies the locus of witnessing and true cognizance of the soul. It was at this moment that we heard, without ears, His exalted words: **Am I not your Lord**, and we responded without a tongue, **yes, indeed.**[13]

In the Holy Qurʾān:

This word is mentioned forty-six times in the noble Qurʾān in a variety of etymological forms. These include the following verses:

12   *Al-Muʿjam al-ʿArabī al-Asāsī*, p. 874.
13   Q Aʿrāf 7:172.

God says: **And [remember] when his Lord tried Abraham with [certain] words, and he fulfilled them. He said: 'I am making you an imam for mankind.' He said, 'and of my progeny?' He said, 'My pact does not include the wrongdoers.'** [14]

God says: **It is not piety to turn your faces toward the east and west. Rather, piety is he who believes in God, the Last Day, the angels, the Book, and the prophets; and who gives wealth, despite loving it, to kinsfolk, orphans, the indigent, the traveler, beggars, and for [the ransom of] slaves; and performs the prayer and gives the alms; and those who fulfill their pacts when they pledge them, and those who are patient in misfortune, hardship, and moments of peril. It is they who are the sincere, and it is they who are the reverent.** [15]

God says: **Yea! Whosoever fulfills his pact and is reverent—truly God loves the reverent.** [16]

God says: **Truly those who sell God's pact and their oaths for a paltry price, they shall have no share in the Hereafter, and God will not speak to them, nor will He look at them on the Day of Resurrection, nor will He purify them. And theirs shall be a painful punishment.** [17]

God says: **[...] Those who fulfill the pact with God and break not the covenant.** [18]

---

14 Q Baqara 2:124.
15 Q Baqara 2:177.
16 Q Āl ʿImrān 3:77.
17 Q Āl ʿImrān 3:78.
18 Q Raʿd 13:20.

God says: **And approach not the orphan's property, save in the most virtuous manner, till he reaches maturity. And fulfill the pact; surely the pact is called to account.** [19]

God says: **They have no power of intercession, save the one who has made a pact with the All-Merciful.** [20]

God says: **Then Moses returned to his people, angry and aggrieved. He said, 'O my people! Did your Lord not make you a goodly Promise? Did the pact seem too long for you? Or did you desire that the anger of your Lord be unleashed upon you, such that you failed your tryst with me?'** [21]

God says: **And We indeed made a pact with Adam aforetime, but he forgot. And We found no resoluteness in him.** [22]

God says: **Did I not make a pact with you, O Children of Adam, that you not worship Satan—truly he is a manifest enemy unto you.** [23]

In the Noble Hadith:

Mujāshi', may God be pleased with him, narrated, "My brother and I came to the Prophet and said, 'Let us pledge allegiance to you for Migration (*hijra*).' He responded, 'The [time for] Migration has come to an end.' I asked, 'Then on what

---

19   Q Isrā' 17:34.
20   Q Maryam 19:87.
21   Q Ṭā Hā Q 20:86.
22   Q Ṭā Hā Q 20:115.
23   Q Yā Sīn Q 36:60.

terms will you accept our pledge of allegiance?' He replied, 'Submission (*islam*) and struggle (*jihad*).'" [24]

Umm 'Aṭiyya, may God be pleased with her, narrated: "We pledged allegiance to God's Messenger ﷺ, and he recited to us: **[O Prophet! When believing women come unto thee, pledging unto thee] that they will not ascribe any partners unto God, [nor steal, nor fornicate, nor slay their children, nor bring a slanderous lie that they have fabricated between their hands and feet, nor disobey thee in anything honorable, then accept their pledge, and seek God's Forgiveness for them. Truly God is Forgiving, Merciful.]** [25] And he forbade us from bewailing the dead, whereupon a woman withdrew her hand and said, 'So-and-so lamented for one of my relatives, so I must repay her in kind.' The Prophet ﷺ did not object, so she went off and later returned to the Prophet ﷺ, who accepted her pledge of allegiance." [26]

Junāda b. Abī Umayyad narrated, "We visited 'Ubāda b. al-Ṣāmit when he was ill and said to him: 'May God restore your health! Narrate to us a hadith by which God will benefit us, and which you heard from God's Messenger ﷺ.' He replied, 'God's Messenger ﷺ called us, and we pledged allegiance to him. His terms included that we hear and obey him whether it be to our advantage or disadvantage, whether in adversity or prosperity, and even when someone is given preference over us, and with-

---

24   Bukhārī, *Ṣaḥīḥ*, K. al-Jihād, #2758.
25   Q Mumtaḥina 60:12.
26   Bukhārī, *Ṣaḥīḥ*, K. tafsīr al-Qur'ān, #4540.

out attempting to usurp authority from those to whom it is entrusted. He said: "except when you see a demonstrable display of unbelief, wherein God provides you with justification [to disobey].""" [27]

Salama, may God be pleased with him, said: "'I gave the pledge of allegiance [of al-Riḍwān] to the Prophet ﷺ, then moved to the shade of a tree. When the number of people around the Prophet ﷺ diminished, he said, 'Ibn al-Akwaʿ, will you not pledge allegiance?' I replied, 'I already did, Messenger of God.' He said, 'Then do it again.' So I pledged my allegiance to him a second time." He was asked, "Abū Muslim, on what terms did you pledge allegiance on that day?" Salama replied, "On our lives." [28]

Yasār narrated: "I can still picture myself on the Day of the Tree, holding a branch over the Prophet's ﷺ head as he took the oath of allegiance from the people. There were fourteen hundred of us. We did not pledge allegiance on our lives, but we pledged that we would not flee from battle." [29]

ʿAbd Allāh b. ʿUmar, may God be pleased with him, said, "'When we pledged our allegiance to God's Messenger ﷺ to hear and obey, he would tell us: 'as well as you are able.'" [30]

---

27 Muslim, *Ṣaḥīḥ*, K. al-Imāra, #3433.
28 Bukhārī, *Ṣaḥīḥ*, K. al-Jihād waʾl-Siyar, #2756.
29 Muslim, *Ṣaḥīḥ*, K. al-Imāra, #3433.
30 Bukhārī, *Ṣaḥīḥ*, K. Tafsīr al-Qurʾān, #6691.

Jarīr b. 'Abd Allāh said: "I pledged my allegiance to God's Messenger ﷺ to perform the prayers, pay the *zakāt*, and offer sincere counsel to every Muslim." [31]

'Ubāda b. al-Ṣāmit, may God be pleased with him, said: "I was one of the chiefs who pledged allegiance to God's Messenger ﷺ. We pledged not to associate partners with God, steal, fornicate, take a life that is forbidden by God, rob, or disobey. Paradise would be our reward if we kept this pledge; but if we were to commit any of these sins, then God would pass judgment upon us." [32]

Mu'āwiya b. Qurra reported that his father said: "I came to God's Messenger ﷺ in the company of a group of people from Muzayna, and we pledged our allegiance to him. His shirt was open, and after we pledged our allegiance to him, I slid my hand into the opening of his shirt and touched the Seal." [33]

In the Sufi tradition:

Following the 2nd/8th century and the earthly departure of the Companions and their Followers, voices began calling people unto renunciation (*zuhd*), abstinence (*taqashshuf*), contenting oneself with the minimum of this world, and attending to the Real. The Sunni masters (sing. *shaykh*) and knowers of God (sing. *'ārif*) who voiced this calling were called "Sufis" by the common believers. This awakening was a call to return to

---

31   Bukhārī, *Ṣaḥīḥ*, K. al-Ṣalāt, #496.
32   Bukhārī, *Ṣaḥīḥ*, K. al-Manāqib, #3630.
33   Aḥmad, *Musnad*, #15275.

the way of the righteous forebears. It was a call to **bear patiently with those who call upon their Lord morning and evening, desiring the Face of God.** [34] It was, and continues to be, a calling rooted in clear insight and colored by the lustrous Light of the Beloved ﷺ.

Two desert Arabs went to the holy Prophet ﷺ. One of them said, "Who is the best of men, Muḥammad?" The Prophet ﷺ replied, "The one who lives a long and virtuous life." The other one asked, "The legislations of Islam are too many for us. What general teaching should we hold fast to?" He replied, "Let your tongue be continuously moistened by the remembrance of God." [35] The remembrance of God is thus the pivotal axis of religious practice. It is the concealed secret (*ṭalsam*) that brings together all the inner meanings and levels of religion. It is the supreme spirit that permeates the entire body of the Law.

God says: He [it is] Who created the heavens and the earth and whatsoever is between them in six days, then ascended over the Throne, the All-Merciful (*al-Raḥmān*); so ask, regarding Him, an informed one (*khabīr*). [36] The term "Shaykh" carries an outward significance and an implied meaning, but few people realize its true measure. Most of those who enter the arena of the Sufis fail to recognize its rightful due. Now the Holy Book mentions the term **"informed one"** (*khabīr*)— so who is this **informed one?**

---

34   Q Kahf 18:28.
35   Ahmad, *Musnad*, #17339.
36   Q Furqān 25:59.

The **informed one** is the one who has tasted the pure meaning of the "ascendance" (*istiwā'*) of the letter *Nūn* of the name *al-Raḥmān* (the All-Merciful), and fully embraced the knowledge that comes from God's nearness (*'ilm ladunī*), so that his spirit ascends above his material body, such that every particle is anointed with the perfume of this majestic Name. The **informed one** is the one who attains realization of the letter *Bā'* of the *Basmala*,[37] and has a firm footing in servanthood. He is the embodiment of this existence, the locus of God's gaze, and the heart of this world. All existing things **rotate within the orbit** of his existence.[38] He is the one in whom all shadows of existence are beheld equally through his spiritual essence. Engendered existence and all that it contains in his presence is like a speck of dust. The **informed one** is the one whom God appoints to be a lantern of Muḥammadan guidance. God establishes him upon the throne of love, endows him with the scepter of courtesy, and gives him direct knowledge of His Name and then renders him its object. This, then, is the **informed one**, and that which remains concealed is even greater.

God says, **for every community, there is a guide;**[39] that is, in every community there is someone who opens peoples' eyes and shows them the Path. Such a person is the guiding lantern, whose lamp draws from the Lamp of God's Messenger ﷺ and is

---

37   The *Basmala* is the formula of consecration and the first verse of Surah al-Fātiḥa: "In the name of God, the All-Merciful, the Ever-Merciful" (*Bismillāh al-Raḥmān al-Raḥīm*).

38   In reference to the verse, *each rotates in an orbit* (Q Yā Sīn 36:40).

39   Q Ra'd 13:7.

lit by a luminous initiatic chain from God's folk. This guide subsists by and for this Light, and is extinguished by God in His presence. God has bestowed upon him the robe of guidance and right conduct, endowed him with the sword of resolve and reverence, and taught him what he knew not. The guide inherits the call mentioned in the verse: **Say, 'O My Servants who have been prodigal to the detriment of their own souls! Despair not of God's Mercy. Truly God forgives all sins. Truly He is the Forgiving, the Merciful.'** [40]

To this effect, the master of our master, Sīdī Aḥmad al-ʿAlawī (d. 1934), may God sanctify his secret, wrote in one of his poems:

The Breath of the All-Merciful hailed
from the Yemen

In the form of a human being
and a spirit from me.

This moment brings me honor:
recognize that I am

Unique in my time
singular in my homeland.

---

40   Q Zumar 39:53.

I am the ink of gnosis
I am the standing citadel

I am the Light in all entities
I am all things besides me

I am the kernel of faith
I am the Pole of the religion

I am not a human being
nor am I of the Jinn

I am the secret of the All-Merciful
I am such that all hails from me

This is why God says: **and follow the way of those who turn in repentance unto Me;** [41] that is, follow the path and the way of the gnostic saints who travel upon the upright Path, and return to Me at every moment in time.

Concerning the Qur'ānic passage:

And We have enjoined man concerning his parents—his mother bore him, weakness upon weakness, and his weaning was two years—give thanks unto Me and unto thy parents. Unto Me is the journey's end. But if they strive to make thee ascribe as a partner unto Me that which thou hast no knowl-

---

41   Q Luqmān 31:15.

edge, then obey them not. Consort with them in this world in a kindly manner, and follow the way of those who turn in repentance unto Me. Then unto Me is your return, and I shall inform you of that which you used to do. [42]

Ibn ʿAjība (d. 1809) says in his commentary, *The Vast Ocean* (*al-Baḥr al-madīd*), that this verse was revealed in connection with Saʿd b. Abī Waqqāṣ, who according to several accounts had always honored his mother, but when he embraced Islam, his mother asked him to leave the faith, saying that if he persisted, she would not eat or drink until she died, and people would all declare his shame by saying that he had killed his mother. After three nights had passed and his mother still had not eaten, Saʿd complained to God's Messenger ﷺ, and the verse was revealed. Some read this verse as addressing the situation of Saʿd b. Waqqāṣ, but understand it as a command to follow the way of Abū Bakr, under whose tutelage Saʿd is reported to have embraced Islam. [43]

Showing loving kindness to one's parents is obligatory, and this is especially the case for spiritual seekers. They must obey their parents in all things, except if they forbid them from the companionship of a Shaykh who trains disciples, for it is he who purifies them from hidden idolatry (*shirk khafī*), [44] a sin from which none is safe, and thus the verse includes the Shaykh in an all-inclusive sense and by way of allusion.

---

42 Q Luqmān 31:14-15.
43 *The Study Quran*, pp. 1002-3.
44 Ascribing partners unto God.

That is to say: this verse tells us that **if they strive to make thee ascribe as a partner unto Me** by following your passions, your personal fulfillment, or your love for them, **then obey them not. Consort with them in this world in a kindly manner, and follow the way of those who turn in repentance unto Me**, a subtle allusion to the Shaykh who trains disciples.

We have previously mentioned Junayd's (d. 910) quote: "My father ordered me to do something, and [my Shaykh] al-Sarī al-Saqaṭī (d. 867) ordered me to do something else, and I prioritized al-Sarī's order, and in that I discovered a great secret."

It is also said that the Shaykh of our Shaykhs, the well-known friend of God, Sīdī Yūsuf of Fez (d. 1604), had a young disciple who was the son of one of the notables of the city, and whose father would prohibit him from visiting the Shaykh and reprimand him for keeping his company. Sometimes the father would even go to the Shaykh's gathering and abuse him. Despite this, the Shaykh would tell the young disciple: "Obey your father in all things, except in coming to see us." [45]

Therefore, you should follow the Path of the righteous. Follow the way of those upon whom the Lights of the Real are manifest; Lights that are perceived at the sensory level, not just at the level of meaning. Leave the objects of the imagination and the senses behind, and follow the way of **the one who submits his face to God, while being virtuous.** [46] Hold fast to

---

45   Ibn ʿAjība, *al-Baḥr al-madīd*, vol. 5, p. 370.
46   Q Baqara 2:109.

him, for he is the secret of your intercession, even though you are unaware of it.

God says: **They are those whom God has guided, so follow their guidance.**[47] He guided them by the Name to the Named, and by the reality of things to the Real. Their Path is made smooth for travel. It is protected and purified from the ambushes of the lower self and from the intrusions of the Devil.

In commenting on this verse, Sīdī Ibn ʿAjība writes:

"These esteemed masters are given superiority in rank over other people of their age by the fact that they are divinely guided to the Lights of divine oneness (*tawḥīd*) and to the secrets of His exclusive singularity (*tafrīd*). Moreover, God singled them out by perfecting both their servanthood and their courtesy toward the magnificence of Lordship. Thus, God's telling his beloved ﷺ to **follow their guidance** opens the door to the attainment of superiority in rank. For whoever takes the prophets as guides will be given eminence among the people of their age. Furthermore, God brought together in His beloved ﷺ what was dispersed among the prophets, and he ﷺ surpassed them in love and in degrees of ascent. He is thus the master of the first and the last, and whoever takes him as his guide in his deeds, words, and moral character will receive mastership in the measure of their emulation of him. Moreover, the divine command for the Prophet ﷺ to **follow them** is with respect to observing

---

47   Q Anʿām 6:90.

courtesy, and that was before he surpassed them in the station by which God singled him out. For Prophets also journey and advance spiritually in a manner that is appropriate to them, just as saints journey and advance spiritually in a manner that is appropriate to them." [48]

In the verse that follows, God says in the Holy Book: **and they did not measure God with His true measure.** [49] Therefore, the one who does not measure God's elect by their measure does not measure God's majesty, and in fact abases that which God exalts, and belittles that which God loves. For they are the true servants. They asked you to feed them, but you refused because of your ignorance, and because of the layers of separative entities (*aghyār*) that have weakened the vision of the eye of your heart. The Messenger of God ﷺ said: "God, exalted and majestic, will say on the Day of Resurrection: 'O child of Adam, I was sick but you did not visit Me.' He will respond, 'Lord, how could I visit you, when you are the Lord of the Worlds?' He will say: 'Did you not know that My servant so-and-so was sick, but you did not visit him? Did you not know that if you had visited him, you would have found Me with him? O child of Adam, I asked food from you but you did not feed Me.' He will say: 'My Lord, how could I feed You, when You are the Lord of the Worlds?' He will say: 'Did you not know that my servant so-and-so asked food from you, but you did not feed him? Were you not aware that if you had fed him, you would have found

---

48   Ibn ʿAjība, *al-Baḥr al-madīd*, vol. 2, p. 281.
49   Q Anʿām 6:91.

that with Me? O child of Adam, I asked you for water, but you did not give it to Me.' He will say: 'My Lord, how could I give You water, when You are the Lord of the Worlds?' He will say: 'My servant so-and-so asked you for water, but you did not give it to him. Had you given him water, you would have found that with Me.'"[50]

These servants did not ask you to feed them out of hunger. They spend their nights with their Lord, who feeds them and gives them drink. Rather, they asked you to feed them so that you may attain through that act something of their proximity to God, and in order to impart something of their fragrance upon you. They offer you their love, even as you try to distance yourself from them. How then can their Light pervade your being, when you have withdrawn from them and strayed from the congregation? You claim to have no need for them and to have no need for intermediaries. Yet you drown in Saul's stream[51] of separation without knowing it. The "I" of your ego has taken total control over you. So come hither, and we will erase your "I" with the identity, the "He-ness", of the Real (*huwiyyat al-Ḥaqq*). No matter how much you distance yourself from us, you only come nearer to us. You refuse to take your oath of allegiance, yet we are your indispensable and inevitable way out. We are the antidote to the venom of your lower self. You need the one who can **pass the camel** of your lower self **through the**

---

50   Muslim, *Ṣaḥīḥ*, K. al-Birr wa'l-ṣila, #4668.
51   Q Baqara 2:249.

eye of the needle of your spirit (*rūḥ*).[52] You cannot flee from us, for we are your original purity.

✿

The Litany (*al-wird*)

In the Arabic language:

The word *wird* means "drink" (*sharb*).

In the Terminology of the Karkariya Order:

The litany (*al-wird*) is a luminous flow that extends from the heart of the Shaykh to the heart of the disciple, by which the Shaykh draws the disciple into a pure, supra-sensory presence. It is the rope that is grasped in order to bring down the spiritual being of the disciple to be watered from the fresh well waters of the Shaykh.

The *wird* is the breeze from Yemen that bears the Breath of the All-Merciful (*nafas al-Raḥmān*).[53] It is the water of life falling from the spiritual clouds of the Shaykh to the bodily earths of the disciple. The *wird* is *widd* (love), and *widd* is one of the seventy thousand degrees of the heart, corresponding to the number of veils between the Real and the creation.[54]

---

52 Q A'rāf 7:40.
53 Al-Bazzār, *al-Baḥr al-zakhkhār*, vol. 9, p. 150.
54 Al-Ṭabarānī, *Kabīr*, #5666.

Anas b. Malik narrated that the Prophet said, "I asked Gabriel, 'Did you see your Lord?' He answered, 'There are seventy veils of Light between Him and me; if I saw just the least of those veils, I would burn.'"" [55]

Abū Hurayra narrated that two men came to the Prophet and one of them asked, "O Abū al-Qāsim, did God veil Himself from His creation by something other than the heavens and the earth?" He answered, "Yes. Between Him and the angels of the throne, there are seventy veils of fire, seventy veils of Light, seventy veils of darkness, seventy veils of sparkling brocade, seventy veils of radiant silk, seventy veils of white pearls, seventy veils of red pearls, seventy veils of yellow pearls, seventy veils of green pearls, seventy veils of gleam coming from fire and Light, seventy veils of ice, seventy veils of water, seventy veils of cloud, seventy veils of cold, and seventy veils of divine majesty that cannot be described." The man added, "Tell me more about the next angel." The Prophet asked, "Do you believe what I have just told you?" He answered, "Yes, I do." The Prophet ﷺ said, "The next angel is Raphael (Isrāfīl), then comes Gabriel, then Michael, then the Angel of Death, may God bless them all." [56]

The *wird* is the primary gate leading to spiritual opening (*fatḥ*). It is the foundation and reference for the disciple. This is why the *wird* must be observed regularly with very great care. It must be done at a specific time, and must not be delayed

---

55   Al-Ṭabarānī, *Kabīr*, #6581.
56   Al-Ṭabarānī, *Kabīr*, #9178.

except when absolutely necessary. The time of the *wird* begins after the dawn prayer and after the sunset prayer. The *dhikr* must be done with concentration, for it the disciple's bond of connection, and to sever it is to sever one's bond with God. In this sense it has been said, "He who has no *wird*, has no *wārid* (divine inspiration)." The *wird* must not be done in a noisy location replete with distractions; instead, it must be done in a quiet and empty room, closing the eyes and calling to mind the unequalled greatness of the Almighty.

In our Order, the *wird* is obligatory until death for all disciples; it is not subject to change either in the form nor in the count.

Imam Ibn ʿAṭāʾ Allāh al-Iskandarī says in one of his aphorisms, "Inspiration (*wārid*) is to be found in the Hereafter, while the *wird* vanishes with the vanishing of this world. It is more fitting to be occupied with something for which there is no substitute. The *wird* is what He seeks from you; the *wārid* is what you seek from Him. Is there any comparison between what He seeks from you and what you seek from Him?"[57]

The sincere disciple forgets his own will and vanishes into the will of his shaykh. The *wird* is the first step leading to that. This means that the disciple will do what his shaykh assigns to him without asking for anything extra, because extra practices can be the cause of misguidance. If he must request something, it ought to be contentment, for that is the ultimate aim of every desire.

57 See Danner's translation of *The Book of Wisdom*, aphorism #112, p. 75.

The fall of the Israelites was caused by their desire for more. They were not content with a single kind of food, and sought to exchange what was better for something that was worse, though they did not realize it. God says: **And when you said, "O Moses, we shall not endure one food, so call upon your Lord for us, that He may bring forth for us some of what the earth grows: its herbs, its cucumbers, its garlic, its lentils, its onions." He said, "Would you substitute what is lesser for what is better? Go down to a town, and you will have what you ask for." So they were struck with abasement and poverty, and earned a burden of wrath from God. That is because they disbelieved in the signs of God, and killed the prophets without right. That is because they disobeyed, and were transgressors.** [58] They descended into the town of their lower selves, and were struck with abasement and the poverty of deprivation and heedlessness.

Be satisfied with what your Lord has granted you; and may God be pleased with a man who knows his worth but is happy to stop short of it. Think about the verse, **covet not that by which God has favored some of you above others.** [59] Be the servant of God, and not the servant of the *wārid* and visions. Do not act like you are the one who is owed something, for this is an accusation and a breach of etiquette. The gnostic aspires to sincerity in worship and fulfillment of the rights of lordship. Be a servant totally devoted to God.

58 Q Baqara 2:61.
59 Q Nisāʾ 4:32.

God sets forth a parable: a man in whom quarreling partners share, and a man belonging to one man: are the two equal in likeness? Praise be to God! Nay, but most of them know not.[60]

The *wird* is part of the servant's courtesy, whereas the *wārid* is a gift from the Lord. The *wird* is what He desires from you; the *wārid* is what you desire from Him. What is your desire next to His? Observe the courtesy of servanthood by offering total service, for that is the proper way to show gratitude for blessings.

Imam Junayd never stopped his *wird* even in the agonies of death. When asked why this was, he answered, "Who better to do it than me, when my book is about to close?" If he never ceased his service even in this state, may God be pleased with him, how could he have ceased it in easier situations?

Imam Junayd was told that some people claimed that they had arrived at a state where they were no longer required to perform their religious duties. He answered, "They have arrived indeed—to Hell!" He added that the case of the libertine, the fornicator, or the thief is less serious than the case of the one who claims that he no longer needs to worship. He was right, because the fornicator and the thief are sinners, but they do not go beyond the limit of apostasy, unlike the one who claims the obligations have been lifted from him, for such a person has been pulled out of the religion like a hair pulled out of a ball of dough.

---

60   Q Zumar 39:29.

Hold fast to this principle, dear brother, and do not listen to those who have studied mystical teachings in books and fallen into heresy and unbelief, imagining capriciously that they are excused from righteous action. The Prophet ﷺ said, "None of you [truly] believes until his desires are subservient to that which I have brought."[61] God says, **Say, "If you love God, follow me, and God will love you and forgive your sins. And God is Forgiving, Merciful."**[62]

You must follow the example of the Prophet ﷺ, as well as the example of the pious predecessors in words, deeds, and states. If you do so, you will gain access to their rank and be rewarded with their company, because everyone in the Hereafter will be with those they loved in this world.

Take care to not belittle the *wird* because of the [perceived shortness of its] length. For the results of *dhikr* are not linked to length, but to a heart free of alterities and purified from turbidities. Saying *subḥān Allāh* with concentration and reverence only one time is better than saying it thousands of times with heedlessness and vain desire. To this effect, Imam Ibn ʿAṭāʾ Allāh says in one of his aphorisms, "Spiritual replenishment (*imdād*) arrives in accordance with preparedness (*istiʿdād*), and the Lights radiate in accordance with the purity of the innermost being."[63]

---

61   Al-Nawawī, *al-Arbaʿūn al-Nawawiyya*, #41.
62   Q Āl ʿImrān 3:31.
63   See Danner's translation of *The Book of Wisdom*, aphorism #113, p. 75.

Let us quote the word of the master of our masters, Mūlāy al-'Arabī al-Darqāwī (d. 1823), may God sanctify his secret, in one of his epistles:

"If anyone wants this noble verse to apply to him, **And thou seest the mountains that thou dost suppose are solid pass away like clouds,** [64] as it has applied to others, he must be content with the smallest amount of this world and he must always wean himself from it and follow the Messenger ﷺ. He must look at his shaykhs, his brothers, and all the servants of God with high esteem. If he does so, then divine inspirations will come to him, God-given knowledge which flows like water with the clouds of mercy, the thunder of mercy, the wind of mercy, the Lightning of mercy, and the coolness of mercy, until the rain of mercy begins to fall onto his heart in every instant. Then there is new knowledge and new action, each sweeter than the last. Peace." [65]

✪

Spiritual Companionship (ṣuḥba)

In the Arabic language:

The word ṣuḥba means to keep another's company, and for two parties to be close to each other.

---

64   Q al-Naml 27:88.
65   Al-Darqāwī, *Rasā'il*, no. 60.

In the Sufi Tradition:

In Sufism, companionship is both in bodily and spiritual. It connects the divine intimacy (lit. with-ness, *maʿiyya*) flowing from the spirit of the accompanied [Shaykh] to the body of the accompanying [disciple]. God says: **The two were in the cave, when he said to his companion, "Grieve not; truly God is with us (*maʿanā*)."** [66]

Spiritual companionship is the key to every good thing that the disciple attains. The Companions reached their spiritual rank only because of their companionship with the Beloved ﷺ. No one can perceive their own faults and what causes them, and so we are all in need of a clear mirror that reflects to us our inner and outer facets. Sayyidunā Abū Hurayra ؓ narrated that God's Messenger ﷺ said, "The believer (*muʾmin*) is a mirror for the believer, and the believer is the brother of the believer. He guards his belongings for him, and defends him from behind." [67]

Therefore, the disciple must follow a lordly companion who has passed away from his lower self, and in whose mirror the name *al-Muʾmin* [the Faithful, or the Source of Safety] has disclosed itself. Such a companion will show the disciple step by step the reality of his own self, so that he can understand its particularities. The disciple needs a companion whose human substance has ceased to exist, and who only subsists by his Lord; a companion who will remind him of God when he looks at him.

---

66   Q Tawba 9:40.
67   Abū Dāwūd, *Sunan*, #4275.

There are several kinds of companionship according to the saintly aspiration and spiritual nature of the disciple. We shall not list them all, but they include the companionship of love, the companionship of training, the companionship of spiritual struggle, the companionship of gazing (*naẓra*), the companionship of the litany, and the companionship of seeking blessings (*tabarruk*). Let us now examine two of these more closely.

The Companionship of Love:

The nature of this companionship is dominated by beauty. The one who experiences it is loved and treated with gentleness and affection. One example of this is the companionship that occurred between the dog and the people of the Cave:

They say, "[They were] three, and the fourth was their dog." And they say, "Five, and the sixth was their dog"—guessing at the unseen. And they say, "Seven, and the eighth was their dog." Say, "My Lord knows best their number; none know them save a few." So dispute not concerning them, save with clear argument, nor consult any of them about them.[68]

Here, God gives us an excellent example of companionship and loyalty whose meanings are beyond the reach of narrow hearts and small minds. God describes the dog in praiseworthy and honorable terms: **with their dog stretching forth his paws at the threshold.**[69] There are indications and deep allusions in this verse for anyone who has a heart and listens attentively.

---

68   Q Kahf 18:22.
69   Q Kahf 18:18.

This dog loves his masters and is entirely extinguished in service of them. Nothing worries him but his master's contentment, and he asks nothing more than to serve him. The dog is totally extinct to the wants of his lower self, and sees only his master's needs. He is glad when his master is glad, and angry when his master is angry. He befriends his master's friends, and opposes his master's enemies. He guards his master's territory without tiring.

His "I" (*anā*) is extinguished in the "he" (*huwa*) of his master. The pronoun "I" is no longer part of his vocabulary; he does not recognize it, and has no desire to. All his language has come down to the letters *hā'* and *wāw* of *huwa*: the numerical value of the letter *hā'* is five, corresponding to the five pillars of Islam, while the numerical value of the *wāw* is six, corresponding to the six pillars of faith. He strives toward the *kāf* of "as if you saw Him" (*ka'annaka tarāh*), for that is the ultimate goal and the final hope. It is the disciple's innermost secret, and the innermost secret is only distinguished from the heart through the *kāf*.

All his being exists through the "he" of his master. His only discourse is "he"; his only speech is "he"; his only expression is "he"; his only allusion is "he." He has melted with love, and he wanders in passion like one who has lost his mind.

The Sultan of Lovers Ibn al-Fāriḍ (d. 1234) said in one of his poems:

It is love, so save yourself, for passion is not easy;
No rational man would choose to be consumed by it.

Live without it, for even love's repose is toil;
Its beginning is sickness, and its end is death.

Yet for my part, to die in the throes of love
Is a gift of life from my Beloved.

Thus do I advise you about love, yet should you ignore me,
I would not blame you; choose for yourself what you desire.

If you would live happily, die a martyr for love;
And if you cannot, then love has its folk.

He who does not die of love has not lived with it;
If you want the bee's honey, you must endure its stings.

Grab the coattails of passion and shed all bashfulness;
Tread not the path of worshippers, though they be noble.

Tell the one who dies of love, "Now you have earned it."
And tell the pretender, "Not all that glitters is gold!"

When the companion-dog was pre-eternally selected for post-eternity, he attained the greatest share. The dog's divine election was on account of his faithful companionship and irreproachable behavior toward his master. He was thus admitted into the Cave of the heart, and the visions of sublime beauty were unveiled for him. He became lost in the Lights of longing, and his spirit soared to the stations of proximity. The tongue of this spiritual state said:

I was alone with the Beloved, while between us
Was a secret more delicate than the blowing breeze.

He allowed my eyes a single glimpse,
And I became known where before I was unknown.

I stood startled between His Beauty and His Majesty,
And my spirit began to express itself.

Turn your gaze to the glories of His Face,
And you will find that the beauty of everything is there.

If all beauty were perfected in a single form,
And then saw Him, it would cry out in rapture.

The Companionship of Spiritual Training:
This is like the companionship between Sayyidunā al-Khiḍr and Moses the Confidant of God ﷻ. Its external aspect is Majesty, while internally it is Beauty. This kind of companionship is beset with trials, and the disciple is required to demonstrate his best behavior and to sacrifice what he loves the most.

Ibn Kathīr narrates the story of this companionship in his exegesis of the Qur'ān as follows:

Ubayy b. Ka'b ﷺ narrated that he heard God's Messenger ﷺ say, "Moses stood up and addressed the Israelites. When asked who the most knowledgeable of all people was, he replied, 'I am.' So God rebuked him, for he was not the font of all knowledge. He revealed to him: 'There is a servant of Mine by the meeting of the two seas who has more knowledge than you.' Moses said, 'Lord, how should I approach him?' He replied, 'Take a fish with you in a basket. When you lose the fish, he will be there.' So he took a fish and put it in a basket, then set off with his servant Jonah son of Nūn ﷺ.

"They came to a rock and lay down to sleep, and the fish wriggled about in the basket and broke free of it, and fell into the sea and began to burrow its way into the water. Then God froze the water around the fish in place so it could not move. When he woke up, his companion forgot to tell him about the fish, so they set off and travelled for the rest of the day and the following night. The next day, Moses said to his servant, **Bring us our meal. We have certainly met with weariness on this journey of ours.**[70] Moses had not felt this weariness until he passed the place where God had commanded him to go. Then his servant said to him, **Didst thou see? When we took refuge at the rock, indeed I forgot the fish—and naught made me neglect to mention it, save Satan—and it made its way to the**

---

70   Q Kahf 18:62.

sea in a wondrous manner!** [71] Moses and his servant were amazed at how the fish had burrowed away. **He said, 'That is what we were seeking!' So they turned back, retracing their steps.** [72] They headed back till they came to the rock, and found a man wrapped in a robe. Moses greeted him with, 'Peace be upon you.' Al-Khiḍr replied, 'Is there really peace in your land, then?' He said, 'I am Moses.' He said, 'Moses of the Israelites?' He replied, 'Yes. I have come to you that you might **teach me some of the sound judgment you have been taught.'** He said, **'Moses, Truly thou wilt not be able to bear patiently with me.** [73] I have knowledge from God which He has taught unto me, and which you know not; and you have knowledge from God which He has taught you, and which I know not.' Moses said, **Thou wilt find me patient, if God wills, and I shall not disobey thee in any matter.** [74] Al-Khiḍr said, **If thou wouldst follow me, then question me not about anything, till I make mention of it to thee.** [75]

"So they headed off along the coast until they came to a ship. They asked them to take them on board, and they recognized al-Khiḍr and took them free of charge. As soon as they were on board, al-Khiḍr pulled out one of the boards from the bottom of the ship. Moses said to him, 'They admitted you on board free of charge, and then **you damaged their ship to drown**

---

71   Q Kahf 18:63.
72   Q Kahf 18:64.
73   Q Kahf 18:67.
74   Q Kahf 18:69.
75   Q Kahf 18:70.

them? You have done a monstrous thing!' He said, "Did I not say unto thee that thou wouldst not be able to bear patiently with me?" He said, "Take me not to task for having forgotten, nor make me suffer much hardship on account of what I have done."[76]

God's Messenger ﷺ said, "The first time Moses did this, it was out of forgetfulness. Then a bird came and alighted on the edge of the ship and dipped its beak into the sea once or twice. Al-Khiḍr said to Moses, 'My knowledge and your knowledge, next to God's knowledge, are like the amount of water this bird took from the sea.' Then they left the ship. As they were walking along the coast, al-Khiḍr saw a youth playing with some others, and grabbed his head and pulled it clean off, killing him. Moses said to him: 'Didst thou slay a pure soul who had slain no other soul? Thou hast certainly done a terrible thing!' He said, 'Did I not say unto thee that thou wouldst not be able to bear patiently with me?' God's Messenger ﷺ said, "This was even worse than the first one." He said, 'If I question thee concerning aught after this, then keep my company no more. Thou hast attained sufficient excuse from me.' So they went on till they came upon the people of a town and sought food from them. But they refused to show them any hospitality. Then they found therein a wall that was about to fall down; so he set it up straight, with his hand. Moses said, 'They refused to feed us or accommodate us. Hadst thou willed, thou couldst

76   Q Kahf 18:72-73.

have taken a wage for it.' He said, 'This is the parting between thee and me. I shall inform thee of the meaning of that which thou couldst not bear patiently.'"[77] God's Messenger ﷺ said, "We wish that Moses had remained patient with him, so that God would have told us the rest of their story."[78]

Contemplate the exemplary behavior of the Confidant ﷺ and how he endured the difficulties and toil of travel to find the one who would help him to increase his knowledge. Where are you compared to the Confidant ﷺ? What is your knowledge compared to his? What is your station compared to his? Despite that, he showed humility and sought knowledge from a servant.

The Beloved ﷺ refers to this slave in the following hadith: "God, exalted and majestic, will say on the Day of Resurrection: 'O child of Adam, I was sick but you did not visit Me.' He will respond, 'Lord, how could I visit you, when you are the Lord of the Worlds?' He will say: 'Did you not know that My servant so-and-so was sick, but you did not visit him? Did you not know that if you had visited him, you would have found Me with him?"[79]

This servant with whom you would find God if you came to visit him is in reality Sayyidunā al-Khiḍr ﷺ himself.

So the Confidant ﷺ asked the permission to begin his companionship with the best manners possible: **"May I follow thee,**

<hr>

77   Q Kahf 18:75-78.
78   Ibn Kathīr, *Tafsīr*, vol. 5 p.175-176.
79   Muslim, *Ṣaḥīḥ*, K. al-Birr wa'l-ṣila, #4668.

that thou mightest teach me some of that which thou hast been taught of sound judgment?" [80] Observe his excellent courtesy and good taste, which provide a role model for every disciple who is blessed with the company of God's folk.

At that moment, the shaykh gives the first test, which is in reality a pre-eternal rule: **He said, "Truly thou wilt not be able to bear patiently with me."** [81] And the disciple answers courteously, **Thou wilt find me patient, if God wills, and I shall not disobey thee in any matter.** [82]

Here we come to an essential question: Why does the disciple say "if God wills," while the shaykh does not? The answer is that the disciple's knowledge is rooted in religious prescription and delimitation, while the shaykh's knowledge is God-given, lordly and non-delimited.

Then the Confidant ﷺ showed even more courtesy by saying that he would not disobey his shaykh's order. The reason for this is that the shaykh's spiritual sustenance, no matter how great, is of no avail if the disciple does not follow his instructions to the letter. The best doctor can do no good if his patient refuses to take his medicine.

Sīdī Ibn ʿAjība wrote:

"The story of Sayyidunā Mūsā with al-Khiḍr is the cause for the manifestation of difference between the exoteric scholars

---

80   Q Kahf 18:66.
81   Q Kahf 18:67.
82   Q Kahf 18:69.

and the esoteric sages. The scholars rectify outward matters, while the sages verify the inward ones. The scholars draw from the ocean of the revealed Laws, while the knowers draw from the ocean of esoteric Realities. It is said that this is the meaning of the Meeting-Place of the Two Seas (*majmaʿ al-baḥrayn*) where Moses, the ocean of revealed Law, met al-Khiḍr, the ocean of esoteric Reality.

We are not saying that Moses did not have any share in the ocean of Reality; on the contrary, he combined both, but God wanted to send him down to the perfection of honor through humility in seeking further knowledge, in order to educate and train him after he had laid claim to power by attributing knowledge to himself. To this effect, Ibn ʿAṭāʾ Allāh says in one of his aphorisms: 'He has prohibited you from claiming for yourself any qualities of created beings that do not belong to you; so would He allow you to lay claim to His Attribute, He who is the Lord of the Universe?'

This, then, is God's way with the elite of His beloved ones; if they ever make displays of power, or stray even a hair's breadth outside the bounds of servanthood, He reprimands them through someone who is lesser in knowledge and status than they are. He does this to nurture and honor them, so that they do not fall below the level of perfection.

For example, we can quote the story of Imam Abū al-Ḥasan Shādhilī (d. 1258) and the woman who said to him, "You brag to your Lord that you have gone hungry for eighty days, while I have not eaten for nine months."

We can also quote the story of Imam al-Junayd and Sarī al-Saqaṭī. In a Sufi gathering, they began to talk about love, each one showing the level he had reached therein. Then a woman in a woolen robe came to the door and repeated back to each of them what he had said. They had displayed the power of their knowledge, so God sent a woman to rebuke them.

The way in which Moses sought al-Khiḍr and travelled to him is a great encouragement to seek knowledge, in particular esoteric knowledge, which is of great importance. Indeed, Imam al-Ghazālī (d. 1111) said that it is a religious duty for every individual, because no one is exempt of faults or sins except the Prophets, upon them be peace. Likewise, al-Shādhilī ﷺ said, "He who does not plunge into this science of ours will die with grave sins to his account, without realizing it." [83]

The jurist Sīdī 'Abd al-Wāḥid b. 'Āshir (d. 1631) said in his famous didactic poem:

He must keep the company of a shaykh, a knower
of the various pathways,
Who will save him from the perils of his journey,

And remind him of God when he sees him,
And help him reach his Master.

---

83   Ibn 'Ajība, *al-Baḥr al-madīd* vol. 3 p. 285.

He must take himself into account with each breath,
And weigh his thoughts with the correct balance;

He must guard over his obligations, which are his capital,
And the voluntary devotions, which are his profit;

He must engage in much invocation with a clear mind,
Seeking help in all this from his Lord;

He must strive against the lower self for
the Lord of the Worlds,
And adorn himself with the stations of Certainty.

He will become with this a Knower of God,
A free man with a heart empty of all but God.

The One God will love him and choose him
For His sanctified presence and make him
among the elect. [84]

And Sīdī 'Abd al-Karīm al-Jīlī (d. 1424) said in a poem:

If fate is kind, and destiny guides you
To a true shaykh, a master of Reality,

---

84   See the last section of Ibn 'Āshir's *al-Murshid al-muʿīn* entitled *Mabādiʾ al-taṣawwuf,* "the first principles of Sufism."

Then do what satisfies him and follow his will,
And renounce all your former desires.

Do not contest anything out of ignorance,
For to contest his will is to rebel against him.

The story of the noble Khiḍr is sufficient—
The youth is slain while the Confidant objects—

Yet when the glow of dawn dispelled the night of his secret,
And he unsheathed a sword to cut the shadows,

The Confidant could only offer his apologies.
So it is with the Sufis and their wondrous teachings.

✦

The Pledge of Allegiance to God

God says, **Truly those who pledge allegiance unto thee pledge allegiance only unto God. The Hand of God is over their hands. And whosoever reneges, reneges only to his detriment. And whosoever fulfills what He has pledged unto God, He will grant him a great reward.** [85]

---

85   Q Fatḥ 48:10.

This is a station that is called "the unity of unity" (*jamʿ al-jamʿ*) because the property disappears into the act, the act into the attribute, and the attribute into the Essence. The property of the pledge manifests through a Muḥammadan attribute within the Aḥmadan reality, so that all considerations and determinations collapse, veils are rent asunder, and human accidents are laid bare at the station of "I become his hand with which he strikes." The Prophet ﷺ was thus the mirror for the most complete, perfect, and perfected manifestation.

Al-Qushayrī says, "There is an explicit declaration of unity-in-itself (*ʿayn al-jamʿ*) in this verse: **and thou threwest not when thou threwest, but God threw.**" [86]

He also said in his *Abridgement* (*Mukhtaṣar*):

"This verse alludes to the complete annihilation (*fanāʾ*) of his blessed being in God, and his complete subsistence through God (*baqāʾ*). For the verse alludes to the station of unity, which is mentioned in the hadith: "And when I love Him, I become his hearing, and his seeing, and his hand, and the rest of his faculties." This, moreover, is the secret of vicegerency and subsistence through God, which is also attained by his ﷺ successors, the knowers of God, the people of annihilation and subsistence. The latter are the people of the prophetic spiritual training in every age. **Those who pledge allegiance to them, pledge allegiance to God; and those who behold them, behold God. He who breaks his pact with them, breaks it to his own detri-**

---

86   Q Anfāl 8:17.

ment: the tree of his spiritual aspiration dries out, and the Light of his inner vision (*baṣīra*) blots out, and he falls back to the station of the common people; the people of the right. However, **those who fulfill that which they have promised God, He will give them a great reward**, namely the perpetual contemplation of His sanctified Essence and the attainment of the station of divine proximity. May God grant us perseverance in the Way of uprightness, without stumbling or backtracking."[87]

No time or place is ever devoid of God's folk and perfected heirs; for they are the locus of the divine Gaze. It is through them that God removes tribulation, sends down life-giving rain, answers prayers, and accepts pious deeds. They are the guarantors of the people of the world.

The pledge of allegiance to a perfected heir is a pledge without intermediary. It is a luminous pledge from the Real to the Real, by the secret of, "I loved to be known." It is a pledge beneath the Tree of the seals of Oneness—a tree beyond location, direction, and spatiality. We said of this in a poem:

The foundation of the Path is the pledge,
With sincerity, resolve, and intention,

Beneath the tree of the divine contentment,
For the birth of the heart.

---

87   Quoted in *Al-Baḥr al-Madīd*, vol. 7 p. 137.

The Lights of the Beloved disclose themselves;
The prophetic spirit,

Which is the supreme veil
The Muḥammadan essence.

God opens the hearts
With this precious sign;

It is the All-Merciful's celestial steed,
To traverse the veils of the unseen.

God was content with the believers when they pledged allegiance unto thee beneath the tree. He knew what was in their hearts and sent down Tranquility upon them and rewarded them with a victory nigh. [88]

God was already content before the **pledge**, for He was **content with the believers** in pre-eternity, and His contentment is one of His attributes, which do not undergo change or replacement because of temporal events. The pledge was one of the fruits of the Tree of Contentment (*shajarat al-riḍwān*), which grew from the seed of God's pre-eternal contentment. A seed of divine satisfaction that let germinate the Muḥammadan tree, **its roots firm and its branches in the sky. It brings forth fruit in every season, by the Leave of its Lord. God sets forth par-**

88   Q Fatḥ 48:18.

ables for mankind, that haply they may remember.[89] The fruit harvested from this tree is a luminous tranquility that is sent down on the sincere servant when he makes the pledge, a tranquility he can behold by the eye of his heart first, then by the eyes of his head, in an awakened state, not in sleep. This is the tranquility of the divine trust and the covenant with God.

Jābir b. ʿAbd Allāh narrated: "Umm Mubashshir told me that she heard the Prophet ﷺ say in the presence of Ḥafṣa, 'God willing, none of the people of the Tree who pledged allegiance beneath it will enter Hell." She said: "O Messenger of God, why not?" He scolded her. Ḥafṣa then quoted: **There is not one of you, but that he will pass over it. It is, with thy Lord, a decree determined.**[90] The Prophet ﷺ replied [by quoting the subsequent verse], "God, the Exalted and Glorious, has said: **Then We shall save those who are reverent and leave the wrongdoers therein, on their knees."**[91]

Al-Baqlī ﷺ said in his commentary on the verse of the pledge: "God was pleased with them in pre-eternity and in His foreknowledge, and His contentment will remain forever, because it is one of His unalterable Attributes without beginning and without end. His contentment is not subject to change due to events or vicissitudes of time, nor because of obedience or

89 Q Ibrāhīm 14:24-25.
90 Q Maryam 18:71. This verse is often understood to mean that each person must cross over the razor-sharp Bridge (*ṣirāṭ*) across the Fire to their final destiny. Others say that it reads: "each will approach *it*," as in the Fire. See *The Study Quran*.
91 Q Maryam 18:72. Ḥadīth from Muslim, *Ṣaḥīḥ* #4559.

transgression. They have been chosen and they remain in this state for all eternity without falling from their level because of slips, nor because of their human nature and passions, for those who are worthy of divine contentment are under His protective care, and the rules that apply to those who are distant from God do not apply to them. They have become characterized by the quality of His contentment and they are pleased with Him just as He is pleased with them. God says, **God is pleased with them, and they are pleased with Him.**[92] This is after He sent down the Lights of intimacy in their hearts as confirmed by the verse: **and [He] sent down Tranquility upon them.**"[93]

God made the descent of the Lights of intimacy as a sign of the validity of the pledge to God and His Messenger. For He knew that there would come a time when some people would claim to possess what they obviously do not, and block the Path for those who sought the Real. So God made the Lights of tranquility as a sign of the authenticity of the chain of transmission (*sanad*) and the Pledge.

To this effect, Sīdī Ibn ʿAjība (may God sanctify his secret) says, "The shaykhs of spiritual training (*tarbiya*) are the Prophet's ✾ successors. He who pledges allegiance to them and commits to follow the Way, pledges to God's Messenger ✾ at the same time. In this sense, we can explain the verse of the pledge: **God was pleased with the believers when they pledged allegiance unto thee beneath the tree. He knew what was in their**

92 Q Bayyina 98:8.
93 Baqlī, *ʿArāʾis al-bayān*, vol. 3 p. 321.

hearts and sent down Tranquility upon them and rewarded them with a victory nigh, and abundant spoils that they will capture; and God is Mighty, Wise.

He was pleased with those who sought His Face when they pledged allegiance to you, O Knower of God, beneath the shadow of the tree of your saintly aspiration (*himma*), and He knew of the sincerity in their hearts, so He sent down Tranquility upon them until they no longer felt the difficulty of the training and spiritual discipline. And He rewarded them with a victory nigh, namely the arrival to the presence of eye-witnessing, and abundant spoils of spiritual openings, unveilings, secrets, and elevation with no limits.

God has promised you abundant spoils that you will capture—then He hastened this for you and restrained the people's hands from you, that it may be a sign for the believers, and that He may guide you upon a straight path—and others of which you were not capable, God has encompassed them; and God is Powerful over all things.

God has promised you, after the spiritual opening, abundant spoils, namely the return to subsistence and to the subsistence of subsistence, the broadening of spiritual stations, and elevation in the ascent of unveilings. He has hastened this for you now, namely the station of annihilation, and retrained the hands of obstacles such as the passions from you, so that you trust your Lord and rely on Him alone. This, that it may be a sign for the believers, those who do not follow the Path but seek guidance through you; and that He may guide you upon

a straight path, the path to reach the presence of holiness and the locus of intimacy. **And He promises other spoils you could not reach** in the herebelow, which He will keep for you until the Day of Judgment, namely the station of, **upon a seat of truth before an Omnipotent King.** [94]

✿

The Hadith of the *Walī*

Abū Hurayra related that God's Messenger ﷺ said, "God has said, 'Whoever aggresses against a friend (*walī*) of Mine, even for Me, I declare war upon him. My servant does not draw near to Me with anything more beloved to Me than the religious duties that I have imposed upon him; and My servant continues to draw near to Me with supererogatory devotions until I love him. And when I love him, I am his hearing with which he hears, his seeing with which he sees, his hand with which he strikes, and his foot with which he walks. If he asks me, I will surely give to him, and if he seeks refuge in Me, I will surely protect him. I do not hesitate about anything that I do so much as I hesitate about his death. For he dislikes death, and I do not like to displease him.'" [95]

---

94 Q Qamar 54:55. Ibn ʿAjība, *al-Baḥr al-Madīd*, vol. 7, p. 144.
95 Al-Bukhārī, *Ṣaḥīḥ* #6050.

Imam al-Nawawī (d. 1277) selected this extremely important hadith in his famous collection of "The Forty Hadiths" that gather the essential foundations of Islam. For his part, Imam al-Shawkānī (d. 1839) wrote a book commenting on this hadith, as did Imam al-Suyūṭī (d. 1505).

The first part of the hadith is colored with divine Majesty, as God speaks upon the tongue of His Beloved ﷺ regarding anyone who shows animosity to one of God's saints, even if this animosity is for God. It means that even if his intention is to defend his faith against what he considers to be an unwarranted innovation and to serve God, God will declare war upon him. No one but God knows the identity of the saints; this is why the following wisdom is one of the founding principles of our Way, "Lower yourself and exalt others."

Do not see yourself as being superior to others, because the secret of predestination is unfathomable, and you do not know who will die with a good end, nor who will have a bad end. Indeed, the case of Sayyidunā Adam and Iblīs is a fine lesson for anyone who would reflect on it. Both sinned, but Adam's sin was the cause of his elevation to the station of prophecy, whereas the Iblīs' sin was the cause of his banishment from God's Mercy. What is pivotal is not the servant's deed, but the judgment of the Lord, for He may become wroth with His servant because of only one sin, and He may be content with another because of only one beautiful deed. God be glorified! No one can measure Him with His true measure!

As for the word *walī*, it is also a name that God gives Himself: **God is the Walī of those who believe. He brings them out of the darkness into the Light. As for those who disbelieve, their protectors are the false idol, bringing them out of the Light into the darkness. They are the inhabitants of the Fire, abiding therein.** [96] He then gave this name to those whom He loves and chooses, saying: **Behold! Truly the awliyāʾ [sing. walī] of God, no fear shall come upon them, nor shall they grieve.** [97]

Thus God made the name *al-Walī* as a description of Himself and an attribute for His servant, so that God's servants have a share of the divine Name *al-Walī*, provided that they leave the darkness of the idols of the self for the Lordly Light of the Truth.

It is this very Light that is denied by hearts that are veiled by heedlessness; hearts that have no taste or awareness of the divine presence. Abū Saʿīd al-Khudrī reported that God's Messenger ﷺ said, "Fear the perspicacity of the believer, for he sees with the Light of God." Then he recited, **Truly in that are signs for those who discern.** [98]

Imam al-Shawkānī writes: "Those who deny that the saints have genuine unveilings that are in accordance with the real world have no grounds for doing so. On the contrary, this a

---

96   Q Baqara 2:257.
97   Q Yūnus 10:62.
98   Q Ḥijr 15:75. Ḥadīth from al-Tirmidhī, *Jāmiʿ* #3072.

door that God's Messenger ﷺ opened, as confirmed in the authenticated hadith reported by al-Bukhārī and Muslim, 'In the communities that came before you, there were people who were inspired (sing. *muḥaddath*). If there were to be any such person in my nation, it would be 'Umar." [99]

Who, then, is the *walī*?

The *walī* is the **foremost in good deeds**, [100] protected by heaven's providential care. He is the one whose breast has been split by the *Alif* of *tawḥīd*, and whose heart has been purified with the Light of faith in the [golden] vessel of Islam. The *walī* has been stripped of all of selfish interest, and he sees none other than his Lord's rights. His selfish interests are extinguished in his rights, and his rights are extinguished in his servanthood, and his servanthood is extinguished in the oneness of the Real. He sees nothing but His beauty, scents nothing but His nearness, and tastes nothing but His pure meanings.

From the eye (*'ayn*) of his heart, appeared the dot of the letter *ghayn*, erasing all alterities and revealing deep meanings and hidden secrets. He sees the entire universe as Light that pours from the oceans of the realm of invincibility (*jabarūt*) to the meadows of the spiritual realm (*malakūt*).

To this effect, Imam Ibn 'Aṭā' Allāh al-Iskandarī says in one of his aphorisms, "The cosmos is all darkness, illuminated only by the manifestation of God in it. Whoever sees the cosmos and does not directly witness the Light within it, or with it, or before

---

99   *Qaṭr al-Walī* p. 256.
100   Q Fāṭir 35:32.

it, or after it, is blind to the existence of the Lights, and is veiled from the suns of gnostic sciences by the clouds of created things." [101]

The pre-eternal Lights are unveiled for him at the very heart of non-existence, and he is brought out from the darkness of separation (*faṣl*) to the Light of union (*waṣl*), and from the darkness of duality (*al-bayn*) to the Light of the entity-in-itself (*al-ʿayn*). The Real crowned him with the crown of Sovereignty and dressed him with robe of dignity. The *Alif* is his sword, the *Hā*ʾ his mount, and the two *Lāms* the reins he holds in his hands.

To this effect, a Sufi poem reads:

*Allāh's Alif is my sword, the Hā*ʾ *my mount,*
and the two Lāms the reins in my hands.

It is my celestial steed when I wish to journey,
and my ascension when I wish to climb to the Lote Tree.

God's Name is my secret, my spirit, my heart,
my hearing, my reason, and the Light of my inner vision.

The kingdom and the Higher Assembly revolve around it,
and all God's servants are replenished by it.

101　See Danner's translation of *The Book of Wisdom*, aphorism #14, p. 49 (with modifications).

God raised him to the locus of direct witnessing and clear-sight. He gave him the knowledge of hearts, and seated him on the carpet of intimacy in the very heart of proximity. Verse: **God raises in degrees those among you who believe and those who have been given knowledge. God is Aware of whatsoever you do.** [102]

Ibn 'Ajība says concerning this verse:

"**God raises those who were given knowledge** of the divine Essence through unveiling and eye-witnessing **seven-hundred degrees** over the expert of the rational sciences, who is himself raised seven-hundred degrees over the ignoramus; and God raises the gnostic seven-hundred degrees over the scholar. So people are divided into four classes: the highest one is the class of the *awliyā'* and the knowers of God, followed by the scholarly class, then the righteous, and then the common believers.

The *awliyā'* are those whom God favors with the encounter of a shaykh of spiritual training until they enter the station of annihilation and subsistence. This shaykh will remove the veil of existents from them until they directly witness the Creator. These, then, are the people who are brought near to God (*muqarrabūn*) and who are sincerely truthful (*ṣiddīqūn*). As for the scholars (*'ulamā'*), they are those who apply their knowledge and are sincerely devoted to God.

Regarding the superiority of the knower of God over the scholar, some people said that the knower of God is above what he says, while the scholar is below what he says. When the

---

102   Q Mujādila 58:11.

knower talks from one of the different stations of certainty, he stands above what he describes, because he traversed it before describing it. The scholar, for his part, only describes it with words. Furthermore, the scholar urges you to action, while the knower rescues you from the plight of witnessing your own deeds. The scholar burdens you with religious prescriptions, while the knower relieves you by guiding you to directly witness the spiritual teachings. The scholar shows you the way to the exoteric forms, while the knower acquaints you with the Essence of the Living, the All-Sustaining. The scholar shows you the way to the secondary causes, while the knower shows you the way to the Causer of Causes. The scholar teaches you to witness the intermediaries, while the knower guides you to the Mover of those intermediaries. The scholar warns you against halting with separative entities, while the knower warns you against halting with the Lights and plunges you into the presence of the Secrets. The scholar warns you against open idolatry (*shirk*), while the knower saves you from hidden idolatry. Those are just a few examples that distinguish the knower from the scholar, and there are others."[103]

God's Messenger ﷺ said, "Whoever travels a path in quest of knowledge, God will help him travel one of the paths of Paradise. The angels lower their wings over the seeker of knowledge, being pleased with what he does. The inhabitants of the heavens and the earth, and even the fish in the depth of the oceans, pray

---

103 Ibn ʿAjība, *al-Baḥr al-madīd* vol. 7 p. 344.

for forgiveness for the knower. The superiority of the knower over the worshipper is like that of the full moon to the rest of the stars in the sky. The knowers are the heirs of the prophets. The prophets bequeath neither gold nor silver, but only knowledge; and he who acquires it, acquires an abundant portion." [104]

This prophetic hadith praises the gnostic who knows God. For the eminence of knowledge depends on its object, and there is no knowledge that is more eminent than the knowledge of God. Knowledge of the Sacred Law and its rulings is eminent knowledge, but the knowledge of God and His attributes and Names is still more eminent. The knowledge of God is the mother of all sciences and is named *'ilm al-ummiyya*, knowledge-unlettered. It is the knowledge of God's Messenger ﷺ, which he bequeathed to God's folk.

God says: **He it is Who has sent down the Book upon thee; therein are clear signs; they are the Mother of the Book, and others ambiguous. As for those whose hearts are given to swerving, they follow that of it which is ambiguous, seeking temptation and seeking its interpretation. And none know its interpretation save God and those firmly rooted in knowledge. They say, "We believe in it; all is from our Lord." And none remember, save those who possess intellect.** [105]

The saint (*walī*) is the one who is **firmly rooted in knowledge**, because his divine knowledge is secure and **clear**, unlike the knowledge of those who follow the authority of others (sing.

---

104 Sunan Abū Dāwūd #3160.
105 Q Āl 'Imrān 3:85.

muqallid). The saint traverses the oceans of the realities of certainty, and gazes into the mirror of spiritual realization. He is not confused by the realities of the *jabarūt* within the realms *malakūt*, nor by the disclosures of the *malakūt* within the forms of the *mulk*. It is he who **knows** the **interpretation** of the secrets, the stations of Lights, and the spiritual allusions. He is the witness, through the spirit, to the secrets hidden in the chronicle of pre-eternity.

✧

The Proper Conduct of *Dhikr*

Abū Mūsā narrated that the Prophet ﷺ said, "The one who remembers his Lord and the one who does not remember his Lord are like the living and the dead." [106]

Abū al-Dardā' narrated that the Prophet ﷺ said, "Shall I not inform you about the best of your deeds, and the purest in the sight of your Master, which raises you to the highest degrees, and is better for you than spending gold and silver in charity, and is better than confronting and fighting against your enemy, striking one another's necks?" The companions answered, "What is it, Messenger of God?" He said, "The remembrance of God." Mu'ādh b. Jabal said, "There is nothing more effective to deliver you from the torment of God than the remembrance of God." [107]

---

106 Bukhārī, *Ṣaḥīḥ* #5957.
107 Tirmidhī, *Jāmiʿ* #3325.

Abū Saʿīd al-Khudrī narrated that God's Messenger ﷺ was asked: "Who will be superior in the sight of God on the Day of Resurrection?" He said: "The men and the women who remember God greatly." The narrator stated: "I asked, 'O Messenger of God, are they superior even to those who fight in the way of God?'" He said: "Even if he wields his sword among the idolaters until it breaks blood stained, those who remember God are superior to him."

Sahl b. Muʿādh b. Anas related on the authority of his father that a man asked God's Messenger ﷺ, "Which holy warriors will be the most greatly rewarded?" He replied, "Those who remember God the most." He said, "And who among those who fast will be the most greatly rewarded?" He replied, "Those who remember God the most." Then he asked about prayer, zakat, pilgrimage, and charity, and to each of them God's Messenger ﷺ replied, "Those who remember God the most." Abū Bakr al-Ṣiddīq ؓ said to ʿUmar ؓ, "The rememberers of God have taken all the good for themselves!" God's Messenger ﷺ said, "Indeed." [108]

Dhikr connects the branch to the root, and returns the spirit to the world of the seed, where it may once more declare, "Indeed you are our Lord!", as it did before: **And when thy Lord took from the Children of Adam, from their loins, their seed and made them bear witness concerning themselves, "Am I not your Lord?" they said, "Indeed, we bear witness"—lest**

108 Ṭabarānī, *Kabīr* #16848.

you should say on the Day of Resurrection, "Truly of this we were heedless." [109] In order to be able to reach this objective and to reap the fruits of *dhikr*, the invoker must always maintain proper conduct (*adab*), [110] and make it his constant companion upon the path.

There are more than seventy thousand rules of conduct for *dhikr*, which may be summarized into twenty rules: five rules before the *dhikr*, twelve rules during, and three rules after.

Before the *dhikr*:
1. Make sincere repentance (*tawba*)
2. Perform ritual ablutions, and apply scent
3. Take a moment of silence and stillness
4. Resolve to invoke while drawing replenishment from the saintly aspiration of the Shaykh
5. Be aware that this replenishment from the Shaykh ultimately comes from God's Messenger ﷺ.

During the dhikr:
1. Make sure the place is ritually pure
2. Face the *Qibla* with the hands on the thighs
3. Perfume the room
4. Wear lawful (*ḥalāl*) clothing

---

109 Q Aʿrāf 7:172.
110 *Adab* refers to prescribed Islamic etiquette: courtesy, refinement, good manners, morals, decorum, decency, humanity.

5. Sit alone in a dark room
6. Close your eyes
7. Call to mind the image of the Shaykh
8. Maintain truthfulness (*ṣidq*) during the *dhikr*
9. Maintain sincerity (*ikhlāṣ*)
10. Empty your heart from everything but God
11. Perform the dhikr as the Shaykh instructed, without any additions or subtractions
12. Focus on the meanings of the *dhikr* IN your heart and tell the shaykh of any visions you may have

After the *dhikr*:
1. Be still and await any inrushes (*wārid*)
2. Examine yourself critically for three to seven breaths until the inrush runs its course
3. Do not drink cold water, as it will extinguish the heat of your yearning for the One you invoke.

✪

The General Litany (*al-Wird al-ʿĀmm*)

All disciples must do the *wird* twice a day, after the dawn prayer and the sunset prayer. Anyone who wishes to remember His Lord and invoke blessings upon his Prophet ﷺ has our permission to recite this *wird* for the blessing (*tabarruk*) of it. As for the one whose soul aspires to attain knowledge of its Creator, to witness His Lights and disclosures, and to be brought out of the darkness of ignorance to the Light of divine knowledge, he must absolutely have companionship with the Shaykh.

The *wird* reads as follows:

Aʿūdhu bi'Llāhi min al-shayṭān al-rajīm,
Bismi'Llāh al-Raḥmān al-Raḥīm.

Al-ḥamdu li'Llāhi Rabbi'l ʿālamīn, al-Raḥmān al-Raḥīm,
Malik yawm al-dīn, iyyāka naʿbudu wa-iyyāka nastaʿīn,
ihdinā l-ṣirāṭ al-mustaqīm, ṣirāṭ al-ladhīna anʿamta ʿalayhim,
ghayri'l maghḍūbi ʿalayhim wa-lā al-ḍāllīn (x7) āmīn.

Bismi'Llāh al-Raḥmān al-Raḥīm, wa-mā tuqaddimū
li-anfusikum min khayrin tajidūhu ʿinda Llāhi
huwa khayran wa-aʿẓama ajran wa'staghfirū Llāh,
inna Llāha Ghafūrun Raḥīm.

Astaghfirullāh al-ʿaẓīm inna Allāh Ghafūr Raḥīm (x3)
Astaghfirullāh (x 99) astaghfirullāh
inna Allāh Ghafūr Raḥīm.

Bismi'Llāh al-Raḥmān al-Raḥīm,
inna Llāh wa-malāʾikatahu yuṣallūna ʿalā al-nabī, yā ayyuhā
al-ladhīna āmanū ṣallū ʿalayhi wa-sallimū taslīmā.

*Allāhumma ṣalli 'alā sayyidinā Muḥammad 'abdika
wa-rasūlik al-nabī al-ummī wa-'alā ālihi
wa-ṣaḥbihi wa-sallim (x99).*

*Allāhumma ṣalli 'alā sayyidinā Muḥammad 'abdika
wa-rasūlik al-nabī al-ummī wa-'alā ālihi
wa-ṣaḥbihi wa-sallim taslīmā.*

*Subḥāna Rabbika Rabbi' l-'izzati 'ammā yaṣifūn, wa-salā-
mun 'alā l-mursalīn, wa'l-ḥamdulillāhi Rabbi'l 'ālamīn.*

*Bismi'Llāh al-Raḥmān al-Raḥīm, shahida Llāhu annahu
lā ilāha illā huwa wa'l-malā'ikatu wa-ulū al-'ilmi
qā'iman bi'l-qisṭ, lā ilāha illā Huwa l-'Azīzu l-Ḥakīm,
inna l-dīna 'inda Llāhi l-islām.*

*Lā ilāha illā Allāh, waḥdahu lā sharīka lah, lahu al-mulk
wa-lahu al-ḥamd, wa-huwa 'alā kulli shay'in Qadīr (x99).*

*Lā ilāha illā Allāh, waḥdahu lā sharīka lah, lahu al-mulk
wa-lahu al-ḥamd, wa-huwa 'alā kulli shay'in Shahīd.*

*Bismi'Llāh al-Raḥmān al-Raḥīm, al-ḥamdu li-Llāh al-ladhī
hadānā li-hādhā wa-mā kunnā li-nahtadī lawlā an hadānā
Allāh, laqad jā'at rusul Rabbinā bi'l-ḥaqq.*

Allāhumma laka l-ḥamd (x3)
Al-ḥamdu li'Llāh wa'l-shukru li'Llāh (x 99 in prostration)
Al-ḥamdu li'Llāh wa'l-shukru li'Llāhi kathīrā

In addition to reciting the *wird* twice daily—after the dawn prayer and after the sunset prayer—the disciples read two *ḥizbs* of Qur'ān daily, along with sūras Yā Sīn, al-Fatḥ, al-Wāqiʿa, and al-Mulk. [Al-Fatḥ and al-Wāqiʿa are typically read in the morning, and Yā Sīn and Mulk in the evening].

✦

The Rosary (*subḥa*)

In the Arabic language:

The word *subḥa* comes from the verb *sabbaḥa,* "to exalt, to glorify, to declare transcendent." *Subḥān Allāh* means "God be glorified!" [111] A *subḥa* or *misbaḥa* is a string of beads used for prayer and invocation. [112]

In the Terminology of the Karkariya Order:

The *subḥa* is the Identity (*huwiyya*) of the Name of the Essence, the secret of the gathering of the divine Names, and locus wherein the flow of the Real manifests. It is an allusion to Lord's transcendence beyond the imperfections of temporal

111 *Al-Muʿjam al-ʿarabī al-asāsī,* p. 603.
112 *Al-Munjid fī al-lugha wa'l-aʿlām,* p. 317.

entities, and the deficiencies of any analogy made by the human intellect.

In the Holy Qur'ān:

The word *subḥa* and words morphologically derived from it occur 97 times in the Holy Qur'ān, including the following verses:

God says: **And when thy Lord said to the angels, "I am placing a vicegerent upon the earth," they said, "Wilt Thou place therein one who will work corruption therein, and shed blood, while we hymn Thy praise (*nusabbiḥuka*) and call Thee Holy?" He said, "Truly I know what you know not."** [113]

God says: **He said, "My Lord, appoint for me a sign." He said, "Your sign is that you shall not speak to the people for three days, save through signs." And remember (*sabbiḥ*) your Lord much, and glorify [Him] at eventide and at dawn.** [114]

God says: **And when Moses came to Our appointed meeting and his Lord spoke unto him, he said, "My Lord, show me, that I might look upon Thee." He said, "Thou shalt not see Me; but look upon the mountain: if it remains firm in its place, then thou wilt see Me." And when his Lord manifested Himself to the mountain, He made it crumble to dust, and Moses fell down in a swoon. And when he recovered, he said,**

---

113 Q Baqara 2:30.
114 Q Āl 'Imrān 3:41.

"Glory be to Thee (*subḥānaka*)! I turn unto Thee in repentance, and I am the first of the believers." [115]

God says: Their supplication therein shall be, "Glory be to Thee (*subḥānaka*), O God!" And therein their greeting shall be, "Peace." And the conclusion of their supplication shall be, "Praise be to God, Lord of the worlds!" [116]

God says: The thunder hymns (*yusabbiḥu*) His praise, as do the angels, in awe of Him. He sends forth the thunderbolts and strikes therewith whomsoever He will. Yet they dispute concerning God, and He is severe in wrath. [117]

God says: Glory be (*subḥān*) to Him Who carried His servant by night from the Sacred Mosque to the Farthest Mosque, whose precincts We have blessed, that We might show him some of Our signs. Truly He is the Hearer, the Seer. [118]

God says: The seven heavens, and the earth, and whosoever is in them glorify (*tusabbiḥu*) Him. And there is no thing, save that it hymns His praise, though you do not understand their praise. Truly He is Clement, Forgiving. [119]

God says: He said, "My Lord! Expand for me my breast! Make my affair easy for me, and untie a knot from my tongue, that they may understand my speech. And appoint for me a helper from among my family, Aaron, my brother. Through

---

115 Q Aʿrāf 7:143.
116 Q Yūnus 10:10.
117 Q Raʿd 13:13.
118 Q Isrāʾ 17:1.
119 Q Isrāʾ 17:44.

him increase my strength, and make him a partner in my affair, that we may glorify Thee (*nusabbiḥuka*) much. [120]

God says: So bear patiently that which they say, and hymn (*sabbiḥ*) the praise of thy Lord before the rising of the sun and before its setting, and in the hours of the night glorify (*sabbiḥ*), and at the ends of the day, that haply thou mayest be content. [121]

God says: We made Solomon to understand it, and unto both We gave judgment and knowledge. We compelled the mountains and the birds to glorify (*yusabbiḥna*) along with David; We did this. [122]

God says: And [remember] Dhu'l-Nūn, when he went away in anger, and thought We had no power over him. Then he cried out in the darkness, "There is no god but Thee! Glory be to Thee (*subḥānaka*)! Truly I have been among the wrongdoers." [123]

God says: Then when he came to it, a call came unto him, "Blessed is the One in the fire, and the one around it. And glory be to God (*subḥānallāh*), Lord of the worlds!" [124]

God says: Truly We compelled the mountains to join him in glorifying (*yusabbiḥna*) at eventide and at the break of day. [125]

---

120 Q Ṭā-Hā 20:25-33.
121 Q Ṭā-Hā 20:130.
122 Q Anbiyā' 21:79.
123 Q Anbiyā' 21:87.
124 Q Naml 27:8.
125 Q Ṣād 38:18.

God says: **And thou shalt see the angels encircling all around the Throne, hymning (*yusabbiḥūna*) the praise of their Lord. Judgment shall be made between them in truth, and it will be said, "Praise be to God, Lord of the worlds."** [126]

God says: **The most moderate of them said, "Did I not say to you, why do you not glorify (*tusabbiḥūna*)?"** [127]

God says: **Prostrate unto Him during the night, and glorify (*sabbiḥ*) Him by night at length.** [128]

In the Noble Hadith:

Imam Suyūṭī wrote a treatise entitled "The Gift: Regarding the Use of the Rosary" (*al-Minḥa fī al-subḥa*), which is one of the epistles in his collection of legal verdicts *al-Ḥāwī li'l-fatāwī*. In it, he collected statements from the works of the hadith masters regarding how the Companions, may God be pleased with them all, used date pits and pebbles as *subḥa* for invocation. We shall quote a few excerpts from this book. For more information, you are welcome to consult the book directly.

Al-Tirmidhī, al-Ḥākim, and al-Ṭabarānī narrated that Ṣafiyya said, "God's Messenger ﷺ once came in and found me invoking with four thousand date pits in front of me to keep count. He said, "Daughter of Ḥuyayy, what is this?" I replied, "I am invoking with them." He said, "I have invoked more than this in the time I have been standing here by you." I said, "Teach me how,

126 Q Zumar 39:75.
127 Q Qalam 68:28.
128 Q Insān 76:26.

O Messenger of God." He said, "Say, 'Glory be to God, by the number of everything He has created (*subḥān Allāhi 'adada mā khalaqa min shay'*)."

Likewise, the *Juz'* of Hilāl al-Ḥaffār, al-Baghawī's *Mu'jam al-Ṣaḥāba*, and Ibn 'Asākir's *Tārīkh* relate via Mu'tamir b. Sulaymān, that Ubayy b. Ka'b related on the authority of his grandfather Baqiyya that Abū Ṣafiyya the freedman of God's Messenger ﷺ used to invoke until midday using a container full of pebbles to keep count. Then he would gather them up, pray, and then go back to them and invoke again until evening.

Ibn Sa'd narrated on the authority of Ḥakīm b. al-Daylamī that Sa'd b. Abī Waqqāṣ used to invoke using pebbles to keep count.

Ibn Abī Shayba reported in *al-Muṣannaf* that Sa'd used pebbles or date pits to invoke.

There is no doubt that many well-known people who are cited as role-models and authorities in religious matters have used the *subḥa*. For example, Abū Hurayra had a string with a thousand knots, and would not sleep until he had used it to make twelve thousand invocations.

Abū Dāwūd narrated in his *Sunan* that Abū Baṣra al-Ghifārī related that an elder from Ṭufāwa told him, "I stayed with Abū Hurayra in Medina, and I have never met anyone who took better care of his guests than he did. One day, I was at his home. He was on his bed holding in his hand a bag filled with pebbles or date pits. There was a black servant below him. He was invoking with them, and when the bag was empty, he would hand it to the servant to refill it, and then go back to his invocation."

It has been said that Abū Hurayra used *mujazza'* date pits, meaning pits that were so much used that they became white on some parts while the rest would stay black.

Al-Ḥāfiẓ 'Abdul-Ghanī reported in the entry for Abū al-Dardā' 'Uwaymir ؆ in *al-Kamāl* that he would invoke one hundred thousand *tasbīḥs* every day. He also reported that Salama b. Sabīb said, "Khalid b. Ma'dān would invoke forty thousand *tasbīḥs* daily in addition to his Qur'ān reading. After he died, during the funeral bathing, his finger began to move as if he was doing *tasbīḥ*."
It seems logical that one hundred thousand, forty thousand, or even a much smaller number than that, cannot be counted only with the fingers, meaning they must have used something to help them keep count; and God knows best.

Abū Muslim al-Khawlānī, God have mercy on him, related that he woke up one night holding his *subḥa* in his hand. Then he saw it wrap around his arm and begin to do *tasbīḥ*. Abū Muslim watched as his *subḥa* rotated around his arm saying, *subḥānaka yā munbit al-nabāt wa-yā dā'im al-thabāt*, "Glory be to You, Grower of the plants, Ever Constant One!" He called to his wife, "Come and look at this amazing thing!" She rushed to him and saw the *subḥa* as it turned and invoked. When she sat down, it stopped.

This story was also reported by Abū al-Qāsim Hibat Allāh b. al-Ḥasan aṭ-Ṭabarī in *Karāmāt al-Awliyā'*.

A Transmitted (*musalsal*) Hadith about the Rosary

Imam Suyūṭī continues:

Al-Qāḍī Abū al-ʿAbbās Aḥmad b. Khallikān related in his biographical compilation, *Wafayāt al-aʿyān*, that he once saw a *subḥa* in the hand of Abū al-Qāsim al-Junayd b. Muḥammad (d. 910). Someone asked him, "Despite your honorable rank, you still hold a *subḥa* in your hand?" He answered: "I used it to reach my Lord, so I will certainly not abandon it."

I have received a hadith regarding this matter with a full chain of transmission. Our Shaykh, Imam Abū ʿAbd Allāh Muḥammad b. Abī Bakr b. ʿAbd Allāh transmitted to me, and I saw a *subḥa* in his hand;

He said: Imam Abū al-ʿAbbās Aḥmad b. Abī al-Majālis Yūsuf al-Bāniyāsī transmitted to me, while I was studying with him and saw a *subḥa* in his hand;

He said: Imam Abū al-Muẓaffar Yūsuf b. Muḥammad b. Masʿūd at-Tirmidhī transmitted to me, when I saw a *subḥa* in his hand;

He said: ʿAbd al-Ṣamad b. Aḥmad b. ʿAbd al-Qādir transmitted to me, and I saw a *subḥa* in his hand;

He said: Abū Muḥammad Yūsuf b. Abī al-Faraj ʿAbd al-Raḥmān b. ʿAlī transmitted to us, and I saw a *subḥa* in his hand;

He said: My father transmitted to me, and I saw a *subḥa* in his hand;

He said: I read under the tutelage of Abū al-Fāḍil b. Nāṣir, and I saw a *subḥa* in his hand;

He said: I read under the tutelage of Abū Muḥammad ʿAbd Allāh b. Aḥmad al-Samarqandī, and I saw a *subḥa* in his hand;

I said, "And you heard Abū Bakr Muḥammad b. ʿAlī al-Sulamī al-Ḥaddād, and you saw a *subḥa* in his hand?" He replied, "Yes."

He said: I saw Abū Nasr ʿAbd al-Wahhāb b. ʿAbd Allāh b. ʿOmar al-Muqrī, and I saw a *subḥa* in his hand;

He said: I saw Abū al-Ḥasan ʿAlī b. l-Ḥasan b. Abī l-Qāsim al-Mutaraffiq al-Ṣūfī, and I saw a *subḥa* in his hand;

He said, I heard Abū al-Ḥasan al-Mālikī saying, when I saw a *subḥa* in his hand and asked him, "Master, you still use a *subḥa*?" He replied, "Likewise, I saw my master al-Junayd (may God sanctify his secret) with a *subḥa* in his hand. I asked him, 'Master, you still use a *subḥa*?' He answered, "Likewise, I saw my master al-Sarī al-Saqaṭī (may God sanctify his secret) with a *subḥa* in his hand. I asked him, 'Master, you still use a *subḥa*?' He answered, "Likewise, I saw my master Maʿrūf al-Karkhī holding a *subḥa* in his hand, and I asked him the same question. He replied, 'Likewise, I saw Bishr al-Ḥāfī with a *subḥa* in his hand, and I asked him the same question. He replied, "Likewise, I saw my master ʿUmar al-Mālikī with a *subḥa* in his hand, and I asked him the same question. He answered, 'Likewise, I saw my master al-Ḥasan al-Baṣrī (may God sanctify his secret) with a *subḥa* in his hand, and I asked him, "Master, despite your tremendous stature and the level of your worship, do you still use a *subḥa*?" He replied, "We used it in our beginnings, and we will certainly not abandon it in our last days. I love to remember God with the heart, with the hand, and with the tongue." [129]

If the use of *subḥa* went against the Sunna of God's Messenger ﷺ, there is no doubt that our masters al-Ḥasan al-Baṣrī, Bishr al-Ḥāfī, Maʿrūf al-Karkhī, al-Sarī al-Saqaṭī, and al-Junayd (may God sanctify their secrets and be pleased with them) would not have used it. They were the most eager of all people to follow the noble Sunna, and they would never have contravened the Sunna of our blessed Messenger ﷺ. Why do some people fight against the use of the *subḥa*, making it their life's cause and *raison d'être?* We are living in an era in which Muslims invoke God too little, and do not yearn to meet Him. Is it wise to accentuate people's distance from God? Would it not be preferable to help people to reach God, step by step?

Gradual progression and the use of intermediaries are a divine wisdom and a fundamental cosmic principle. Differences of opinion in secondary matters of the revealed Law are a mercy and an ease for the Muslim community. No legal opinion about the *subḥa* can be any more than a matter of personal reasoning (*ijtihād*), since there is no direct textual evidence to resolve the matter. However, love, kindness, and mutual aid between Muslims are obligations. We must not abandon

---

129 Suyūṭī, *al-Ḥāwī lil-fatāwī, al-minḥa fī al-subḥa*, vol. 2, pp 4-5.

primary concerns for the sake of secondary ones, may God have mercy on you all.

Justification of the Rosary

According to a famous rule in *fiqh*, everything is lawful until proven unlawful.

Thus, anyone who has a good heart and an ounce of intelligence would understand that nothing in the Sunna forbids the use of the *subḥa*; on the contrary, the Sunna orders each Muslim to make *dhikr* in abundance.

ʿAbd Allāh b. Busr said: "A Bedouin man came to the Prophet ﷺ and said, 'O Messenger of God, the Laws of Islam are too many for me, so tell me something comprehensive to which I can cling.' The Prophet ﷺ replied, 'Keep your tongue moist with the remembrance of God.'" [130]

Abū Hurayra reported that God's Messenger ﷺ was travelling along the path leading to Mecca when he happened to pass by a mountain called Jumdān. He said: "Proceed on, it is Jumdān. The *mufarridūn* [131] have gone ahead." They said, "O Messenger of God, who are the *mufarridūn*?" He said, "They are the men and women who remember God much." [132]

---

130 Ibn Mājah, *Sunan* #3791.

131 Translator's note: A *mufarrid* can mean someone who is single-minded or singled out. It should be noted, moreover, that while *tawḥīd* means to declare God's oneness, *tafrīd* means to proclaim God's exclusive singularity. Hence, the *mufarridūn* in Sufi texts can mean those who realize the highest level of *tawḥīd* and abandon themselves in God.

132 Muslim, *Ṣaḥīḥ* #4841.

To this effect, God describes the hypocrites as those who only remember God a little. The one who remembers God often therefore distinguishes himself from their qualities. This is why the Surah of the Hypocrites (*al-Munāfiqīn*) concludes with a command to remember God, and states that the believer is not distracted from the remembrance of God by wealth or children, and that if someone is distracted from God's remembrance by those two things, he will be among the losers.

Al-Rabīʿ b. Anas related that one of the Companions said: "The sign of love for God is the abundance of His remembrance, because the more you love something, the more you remember it."

Fatḥ al-Mawṣilī said: "The lover of God never ceases to remember Him, even for the blink of an eye."

Dhū al-Nūn said, "When someone busies his heart and tongue with the remembrance of God, God casts the Light of yearning for Him into his heart."

Ibrāhīm b. al-Junayd said, "It used to be said that one of the signs of love for God is His continual remembrance by the heart and the tongue. The more someone strives to remember God, the more his love for God will increase."

One of the early Muslims said in his prayers, "Though fools may tire of their foolery, Your lovers never tire of calling upon You and remembering You."

Abū Jaʿfar al-Miḥwalī said: "The heart of the *walī* who loves God is never devoid of his Lord's remembrance, and he never tires of serving Him."

ʿĀʾisha narrated that the Prophet ﷺ remembered God at all times: when he was standing, when he was walking, when he was lying, when he was seated, whether in a state of ritual purity or not.

Misʿar said, "The creatures of the sea keep silent, but Yūsuf never ceased remembering God in prison."

Abū Hurayra had a cord with a thousand knots, and he did not sleep before using it to invoke. Khalid b. Maʿdān would invoke forty thousand *tasbīḥs* daily in addition to his Qurʾān recital. After he died, during the funeral bathing, his finger began to move as if he was doing *tasbīḥ*.

ʿAbd al-ʿAzīz b. Abī Rawwād said: "There was a woman in Mecca who made twelve thousand *tasbīḥ* daily. After she died, during the burial she disappeared from the hands of the men who were carrying her."

Al-Ḥasan al-Baṣrī would often say when he was not engaged in conversation or in any task, *subḥān Allāh al-ʿaẓīm*, "Glory be to God, the Almighty." Someone told a jurist from Mecca about this, and he replied, "Your companion is certainly a learned man. Anyone who repeats these words seven times will have a house built for him in Paradise."

Likewise, the biggest part of Ibn Sīrīn's dhikr was, *subḥān Allāh al-ʿaẓīm, subḥān Allāh wa-biḥamdihi*, "Glory be to God, the Almighty; glory be to God, and may He be praised."

When people were sleeping, al-Mughīra b. Ḥakīm al-Ṣanʿānī would go down to the sea and stand in the water remembering God with the creatures of the ocean.

A man who slept in the house of Ibrāhīm b. Adham said: "Each time I woke up during the night, I saw him invoking God. I regretted that I could not do the same, then I consoled myself with the verse: **That is the Bounty of God, which He gives to whomsoever He will.**" [133]

So the pure Sunna and the Holy Qur'ān encourage us to remember God in abundance, and did not limit this to a particular month as for fasting, nor to particular days as for the pilgrimage, nor to certain times as for the prayers. Rather, remembrance is nondelimited, just as the One Remembered is nondelimited. God says: **O you who believe! Remember God with frequent remembrance, and glorify Him morning and evening. He it is Who blesses you, as do His angels, that He may bring you out of darkness into Light. And He is Merciful unto the believers.** [134]

Frequent remembrance means remembrance done continuously without cease; it is the heart-centered remembrance of the one who is constantly consoled by witnessing the intimacy of the divine Lights, and keeps vigil in the presence of the Real, and wanders in the Lights of divine proximity. His mind never turns from the spirit of the Beloved, nor from the evocation of the innermost secret.

According to Abū Saʿīd, God's Messenger ﷺ said, "Remember God so much that people say you are mad." [135]

---

133   Q Jumuʿa 62:4. Abridged from *Jāmiʿ al-ʿulūm wal-l-ḥikam*, pp 517-518.
134   Q Aḥzāb 33:41-43.
135   Aḥmad, *Musnad* #11461.

The true remembrance begins with the dawn of the heart and continues until the setting of the sun of the spirit. Its different levels are remembrance with tongue, then with the heart, then with the spirit and finally with the innermost secret. The *subḥa* is one of the conditions for remembrance for the Sufis because of its clear advantages and the secrets and hidden meanings it contains. First, the *subḥa* helps with counting, in particular for those who have undertaken to invoke in large quantities that would be unrealistic to count on the fingers. The *subḥa* is also the symbol of the letter *Hāʾ* of the all-encompassing Name *Allāh*. When the disciple looks at the *subḥa*, he remembers his Creator and how he has no power or strength except in God. Its shape is circular like the number zero, which represents extinction. The number of beads is equal to the Most Beautiful Names (99). Many more secrets could be mentioned about the *subḥa*, but this is not the purpose of this book.

God says: **I did not create jinn and mankind, save to worship Me.** [136] Sayyidunā Ibn ʿAbbās said that "to worship Me" here means "to know Me." But it is only with frequent remembrance of God that we can come to know Him. Frequent remembrance necessitates the use of the *subḥa* to keep count, and the rule states that "if something is necessary to fulfill an obligation, then it is itself obligatory."

136 Q Dhāriyāt 51:56.

Reply to Arguments Against the Use of the *Subḥa*:

The following text comes from *al-Mawsūʿa al-Kasnazāniyya*:

Some people have denounced the use of the *subḥa* with weak arguments that we will now summarize and refute.

They argue that God's Messenger ﷺ counted the number of *tasbīḥ* with his fingers because the fingers will testify on the Day of Judgment. They base their argument on two hadiths. One is reported by Abū Dāwūd: "He counted his *tasbīḥ* with his right hand," and the other by al-Tirmidhī: "He counted his *tasbīḥ* with his hand."

Now, even if the Prophet ﷺ did use his hand to count his *tasbīḥ*, the fact remains that he did not prevent his Companions from using date pits, pebbles, or other things to invoke. Moreover, whether a *subḥa* is used or not, it is the same hand that counts the *tasbīḥ*. Therefore, the use of the *subḥa* does not prevent the testimony of the fingers on the Day of Judgment, because they held the *subḥa* and so will not be deprived the Light that emanated upon them during the invocation.

We can quote Imam Suyūṭī's words: "If the invoker is certain that he will not make mistakes when counting his invocations, then counting with his fingers is better. Otherwise, it is better to use the *subḥa*."

They also claim that the use of the *subḥa* leads to showing off and ostentation. For them, giving up the use of the *subḥa* would be better and safer for the faith. Yet showing off can affect us in all our pious deeds—does this mean that we should give up all pious deeds, lest we fall into ostentation?

They argue that it is an innovation that neither God's Messenger ﷺ nor the Companions did, and that every innovation is misguidance, and every misguidance is in Hell.

But God's Messenger ﷺ is reported to have said, "He who inaugurates a good practice earns the reward of it, and of all who perform it after him until the Day of the Judgment." Therefore, scholars judged that it was wrong to systematically consider all new things as misguidance, and that innovations or new things are divided into four categories.

Some innovations are obligatory (*wājib*), such as the establishment and teaching of the study of the Arabic language; others are recommended (*mandūb*), such as building schools; others are unlawful (*ḥarām*), such as mispronouncing the Holy Qur'ān in a way that renders its words into something other than their proper Arabic forms; and some are permitted (*mubāḥ*), such as serving food on a dining table.

Ibn al-Ḥajar said in *Sharḥ al-mishkāt*, "The command to invoke with specific numbers implies that it is recommended to use a *subḥa*, and the claim that this is an innovation is unsound."

Some of them even said that making an exact number of *tasbīḥ* itself is an innovation, so what of counting them with a *subḥa*? To refute this, it is sufficient to refer such people to the hadiths and traditions that clearly mention that some Companions had regular litanies, such as Sayyidunā Abū Hurayra with his 12,000 *tasbīḥ*, or Sayyidunā Khālid b. Ma'dān with his 40,000, or Abū Dardā' with his 100,000. Likewise, some Followers (*tābiʿūn*) had a *wird* with 30,000 *tasbīḥ* and others had a daily *wird* with 300, 600, or 1000 cycles of prayer. [137]

Wearing the *Subḥa* Around the Neck

God says: **God has made the Kaʿbah, the Sacred House, a support (qiyām) for mankind, and the sacred month, and the sacrificial offerings, and the garlands this that you might know that God knows whatsoever is in the heavens and whatsoever is on the earth, and that God is Knower of all things.** [138]

Al-Ṭabarī said in his commentary on this verse:

God made these four things "**supports (*qiyām*) for mankind,**" meaning the *qawām* upon which their affairs stand. Although different interpretations have been given for this term, they all mean essentially the same thing, which is that the *qawām* of a thing is that which safeguards its interests. For example, the sovereign king is the *qawām* of his subjects and those under his authority, because he directs their affairs, protects them from one another's injustice, and defends them against attacks from outside.

Likewise, **the Kaʿbah,** the sacred month, **the sacrificial offerings, and the garlands** (*qalāʾid*) were the **supports** that safeguarded the Arabs' interests during the pre-Islamic age of ignorance; and in Islam too, they served as symbols for the pilgrimage and its rites, and the direction for prayer so that the Muslims could fulfill their obligations.

137 *Al-Mawsūʿa al-Kasnazāniyya,* Letter Sīn, p. 28.
138 Q Māʾida 5:97.

These were inviolable codes that God preserved among the people during the pre-Islamic time, in such a way that someone who committed the worst crimes would fear nothing as long as he was in the sacred enclosure of the pilgrimage. For example, if someone met the murderer of his own father during the sacred month, he would not threaten him. Furthermore, when someone went out with the intention to make the pilgrimage, he would wear a **garland** made of fur around his neck. This **garland** showed people his intention to fulfill his religious duty, and so no one would disturb him.

Once the pilgrimage was done, on his way back, he would wear around his neck another **garland** made of grass or the branches of an arid tree, to protect him from people until he arrived home. These are inviolable codes that God has preserved since pre-Islamic times."[139]

So in pre-Islamic times, it was sufficient for those who were going to the pilgrimage to wear around their neck a special **garland** recognizable by all to avoid being disturbed on their way. This shows that it is lawful for people devoted to religion and worship to identify themselves in a way that protects them from evil people. The intention is to protect ourselves from what might endanger us, whether physically or spiritually.

Furthermore, the *subḥa* that we wear around the neck is for us similar to the ring worn around the finger. The ring refers to authority and power, the *subḥa* to divine proximity. God says:

139 Ṭabarī, *Tafsīr*, vol. 9 p. 9.

We did indeed create man, and We know what his soul whispers to him; and We are nearer to him than his jugular vein. [140]

God used the **jugular vein** as an example of His proximity, because it is the most important vein in the human body and because it is directly linked to the heart, and to the aorta, which causes death when it is cut. Since the **jugular** is inside the body, we can observe that God is closer to us than we are to ourselves. To this effect, a tradition says, "He who knows himself, knows his Lord."

From the perspective of unity-in-itself (*'ayn al-jam'*), nothing exists apart from Him. From the perspective of the separation-in-itself (*'ayn al-farq*), it is a property that subsists through an act, an act that subsists through an attribute, and an attribute that subsists through an Essence.

The jugular vein is on the neck, and this is why God's folk wear the symbol of the Identity (*huwiyya*) of the Name *Allāh* around their necks. Indeed, the *subḥa* is none other than the letter *Hā'* of the Name, and it is in this way that the disciples come to realize the sensory and suprasensory meanings of the aforementioned verse.

Moreover, the neck is a mark of nobility and eminence on the Day of Resurrection, because God made it a sign of faith and spiritual elevation. Muʿāwiya narrated that God's Messenger ﷺ said: "The muezzins will have the longest necks on the Day of Resurrection." [141] Now the azan is in reality a perfect summons;

---

140 Q Qāf 50:16.
141 Muslim, *Ṣaḥīḥ* #585.

and the only summons that is perfected is the summons of those who are worthy of the Name, the perfected spiritual masters, may God sanctify their secrets.

Wearing the *subḥa* around the neck, moreover, is an expression of reverence for the *dhikr* in our hearts, by way of proximity through divine providence (*tawfīq*), not prescription (*tawqīf*). For by wearing it around the neck, one protects the *subḥa* from being lost or damaged; and if the principle is lawful, anything branching from it must also be lawful.

Furthermore, the *subḥa* is the tool of the holy war against the lower self (*jihād al-nafs*). Just as the sword used to fight the enemy is worn at the waist, the *subḥa* is worn at the neck and is used for the greatest holy war, which is to fight an enemy who never leaves us.

Lastly, it should be mentioned that it is quite common for people to wear various things around the neck such as bags, water-bottles, purses, and other things to help with their daily lives; and the *subḥa* is certainly more important than any of those.

2.

The Sacred Dance (*al-ḥaḍra*)

In the Arabic language:

The word *ḥaḍra* means "presence or proximity."[142] The word *raqṣ* (dance) means "to shake and move the body to the rhythm of music or song."[143]

In the Terminology of the Karkariya Order:

It is the symbol of the Shuʻayb-heart that brings together all cosmic manifestation-sites and human realities upon the carpet of direct witnessing, proximity, and the unveiling of the protective robe by the disclosures of the Lights of pre-eternity.[144]

---

142 *Al-Muʻjam al-ʻarabī al-asāsī* p. 327.

143 Ibid p. 541.

144 Translator's note: In the Shaykh's teachings, each prophet has a presence that is specific to him, and Shuʻayb's presence is that of the heart that has perfected the branches of faith (shuʻab al-īmān). The circle of the sacred dance, moreover, represents the circular Hāʼ of the divine Name Allāh or the perfected heart. The Shaykh, or God's vicegerent (khalīfa), stands at the center of the sacred dance and brings together all "cosmic manifestation-sites" and the "realities" of the Perfect Man. These realities are discovered by the disciple through the parting of the veil by which God protects these pure meanings and Lights of pre-eternity from the eyes of the heedless. (With thanks to Muhammad Amine Ghazi for his comments).

The *Ḥaḍra* in the Holy Qur'ān:

God says: Those who remember God standing, sitting, and lying upon their sides, and reflect upon the creation of the heavens and the earth, "Our Lord, Thou hast not created this in vain. Glory be to Thee! Shield us from the punishment of the Fire. [145]

God says: When you have completed the prayer, remember God, standing, sitting, or lying on your sides. Then when you are secure, observe proper prayer, for prayer at fixed hours is prescribed for the believers. [146]

God says: God has sent down the most beautiful discourse, a Book consimilar, paired, whereat quivers the skin of those who fear their Lord. Then their skin and their hearts soften unto the remembrance of God. That is God's Guidance, wherewith He guides whomsoever He will; and whomsoever God leads astray, no guide has he. [147]

God says: Had We made this Quran descend upon a mountain, thou wouldst have seen it humbled, rent asunder by the fear of God. These are the parables We set forth for mankind, that haply they may reflect. [148]

God says: And when Moses came to Our appointed meeting and his Lord spoke unto him, he said, "My Lord, show me, that I might look upon Thee." He said, "Thou shalt not see

---

145   Q Āl 'Imrān 3:191.
146   Q Nisā' 4:103.
147   Q Zumar 29:23.
148   Q Ḥashr 59:21.

Me; but look upon the mountain: if it remains firm in its place, then thou wilt see Me." And when his Lord manifested Himself to the mountain, He made it crumble to dust, and Moses fell down in a swoon. And when he recovered, he said, "Glory be to Thee! I turn unto Thee in repentance, and I am the first of the believers." [149]

The *Ḥaḍra* in the Sunna:

Anas b. Mālik said, "The Abyssinians performed in front of God's Messenger ﷺ, dancing and chanting. God's Messenger ﷺ asked, 'What are they saying?' They replied, 'They are saying, *Muḥammad is a righteous man!*'" [150]

'Alī ؓ said: "I visited the Prophet with Ja'far and Zayd. The Prophet said to Zayd, 'You are my freedman', whereupon Zayd began to hop (*ḥajila*) around the Prophet. The Prophet then said to Ja'far, 'You resemble me in both appearance and character', whereupon Ja'far began to hop behind Zayd. The Prophet then said to me, 'You are from me, and I am from you', whereupon I began to hop behind Ja'far." [151]

Ibn Ḥajar al-'Asqalānī explained that *ḥajila* means to hop on one leg, a kind of dancing. [152]

Ibn 'Abbās narrated a long hadith about how Ali b. Abī Ṭālib, Ja'far, and Zayd disagreed on who had the better right to help a

---

149 Q A'rāf 7:143.
150 Aḥmad, *Musnad* #12303.
151 Ibid #835.
152 *Fatḥ al-Bārī* 7/583.

woman who had been rescued from the idolaters in Mecca. God's Messenger ﷺ, who was present, ruled in favor of Sayyiduna Ja'far. The hadith expert Muḥammad b. 'Umar al-Wāqidī (d. 823) said: "When he ﷺ ruled in favor of Ja'far, Ja'far began to hop on one leg around God's Messenger ﷺ. He asked him what he was doing, and he replied, 'O Messenger of God, when the Negus made someone happy, that person would stand and hop on one leg around him.'" [153]

It was narrated that 'Abd Allāh b. 'Umar said: "I heard God's Messenger ﷺ say on the pulpit: 'The Compeller will seize His heavens and His earths in His Hand' – and he clenched his hand and started to open and close it – 'then He will say: "I am the Compeller, I am the King. Where are the tyrants? Where are the arrogant?"' God's Messenger ﷺ began to lean to his right and his left, until I could see the pulpit shaking at the bottom, and I thought that it would fall along with God's Messenger ﷺ." [154]

Qatāda related on the authority of Anas ibn Mālik that the Prophet ﷺ was climbing Uḥud with Abū Bakr, 'Umar, and 'Uthmān when the mountain began to quake beneath them. He said, "Be still, Uḥud, for upon you stand a Prophet, a man of true faith, and two martyrs!" [155]

Sayyiduna 'Alī (may God ennoble his countenance) said: "I saw the Companions of God's Messenger, and nowadays I find none comparable to them. I swear by God, when the morning

153 Al-Bayhaqī, *Dalā'il*, #1710.
154 Ibn Mājah, *Sunan* #4273.
155 Bukhārī, *Ṣaḥīḥ* #3423.

came, they had pale faces, disheveled hair, and dusty bodies. Between their eyes were the marks of their prostration, after spending the night reciting the Book of God and praying. Whenever God was remembered, they would rock back and forth like the tree in the wind. By God, their eyes shed so many tears that their clothes were wet." [156]

Anas ﷺ related that the Prophet ﷺ said, "The one who has these three will taste the sweetness of faith: that God and His Messenger are more beloved to him than anything else; that he loves another man for the sake of God and nothing else; and that he would hate to return to unbelief just as he would hate to be thrown into fire." [157]

✦

The Basis of the Ḥaḍra

The *ḥaḍra* is one of the allusions of the Sufi Tribe. It symbolizes the gathering of the divine Names within the *Hā'* of the all-encompassing Name of the Essence. For those whose inner vision is opened by the *kāf* of *ka'annaka tarāh*, "as if you saw Him," it symbolizes the eternal Handful (*qabḍa abadiyya*) that discloses itself through the pre-eternal beauty of the Real. For them, the spiritual world has thus become the material world,

156 Abū Nuʿaym, *Ḥilyat al-awliyā'* 1/118.
157 Bukhārī, *Ṣaḥīḥ* #15.

and the unseen has become visible, so that they taste the exquisite bliss of nearness and savor the fragrant breeze of arrival.

Mount Uḥud shook with rapture, yearning, and joy beneath the footsteps of the Beloved ﷺ. It quaked in awe of the Muḥammadan beauty until God's Messenger ﷺ calmed it. Abū Ḥumayd al-Sāʿidī related, "On our way back from the expedition of Tabūk in the company of the Prophet ﷺ, when we arrived near Medina, he said, 'This is Ṭāba, and this is Uḥud, a mountain that loves us, and we love it.'" [158] It is thus clear that Uḥud's tremors were caused by none other than love. Quivering and swaying, then, are among the disclosures of faith. To this effect, a poet has said:

Do not blame Uḥud for shaking beneath him,
For ecstasy is an involuntary ailment.

Uḥud is beyond reproach, for it is a lover,
And passion is never as intense as when the beloved arrives.

In reality, trembles are expressions of the surging waves of love. They come about when one plunges into the cold ocean of yearning. These trembles are accompanied by quivering, tears, fearfulness, shivers, being thunderstruck, fainting, and such things.

158 Ibid, # 4097.

Do you not see that even the stones hurl themselves from heights and fall down in fear joy, love, and yearning for God? **Then your hearts hardened thereafter, being like stones or harder still. For indeed among stones are those from which streams gush forth, and indeed among them are those that split and water issues from them, and indeed among them are those that crash down from the fear of God. And God is not heedless of what you do.** [159]

Just as different musical scales of the voice are subtly linked to the levels of the spirit, trembling and swaying are innate reactions to beautiful sounds, even for animals and inanimate objects—and an inanimate object is really none other than the one who has no heart to feel the flow of pure meanings. Thus God gave us an example in the Qur'ān: **Had We made this Quran descend upon a mountain, thou wouldst have seen it humbled, rent asunder by the fear of God. These are the parables We set forth for mankind, that haply they may reflect.** [160]

If even the **mountain**, despite its boundless strength and rigidity, would have reacted with humility and fear if the Qur'ān had been sent down upon it, then what should the state of the Sufis be in such circumstances?

The state of divine nearness and arrival is utterly irresistible, even to mighty **mountains**. Ibn Taymiyya (d. 1328) told us of this in his collection of legal opinions (*al-Fatāwī*): "When Imam Aḥmad was asked about this, he answered, 'The Qur'ān

159 Q Baqara 2:74.
160 Q Ḥashr 59:21.

was being read in Yaḥyā b. Saʿīd al-Qaṭṭān's (d. 873) presence when he fainted. If anyone were able to resist such a thing, it would be Yaḥyā, for I never encountered anyone more intelligent than him.' Something similar was related from Imam Shāfiʿī, and a similar story about ʿAlī b. al-Fuḍayl b. ʿIyāḍ (d. 803) is well-known. In sum, there are many such accounts from people whose sincerity is not to be doubted." [161]

Ibn Taymiyya's student, Ibn Qayyim (d. 1350), also wrote about the issue of spiritual states (*ḥāl*) in his work, "The Degrees of the Wayfarers" (*Madārij al-sālikīn*), saying: "There is a disagreement on the issue of inducing spiritual ecstasy (*tawājud*) and whether or not it is allowed. Scholars are divided into two groups. The first group say that it is not permitted because it amounts to artifice and pretension. The others say it is permitted for sincere people who wish to be moved to ecstasy by valid spiritual experiences. In this vein, the Prophet ﷺ said, 'Weep, and if you cannot weep, then induce a state of weeping.' In conclusion, if a person seeks to induce ecstasy artificially for the sake of worldly benefit, passion, or ego, he should not be indulged in this. On the other hand, if someone does it in order to trigger a spiritual state or a station before God, he should be allowed to do so. This depends on the person and what is known of his truthfulness and sincerity." [162]

He also said: "If all the pleasures experienced by all the people in the world were attained by a single man, it would be nothing

---

161 Ibn Taymiyya, *Majmūʿ al-fatāwī* 11/7.
162 Ibn Qayyim, *Madārij al-sālikīn* 3/324.

compared to the bliss of a man whose heart is entirely focused on God, joyous in Him, consoled by His nearness, and yearning for His encounter. Only the one who tastes this will believe it, because only the one who experiences what you experience will believe you. May God be pleased with the poet who said:

My friend, do you not see their fire?
He answered: You see what I see not;

Passion has quenched your thirst but not mine,
And so you see in your heart what I cannot see. [163]

Imam Ghazālī, the Proof of Islam, affirmed this when he said about ecstasy (*wajd*): "This may occur because of joy or yearning, and its legal status depends on its cause. If the nature of his joy is noble, and if dance increases it, then it is noble. If the nature of his joy is lawful, then so is the dance. If the nature of his joy is dishonorable, then so is the dance." [164]

Qāḍī ʿIyāḍ related in his work, "The Antidote" (*al-Shifā*), that when the Prophet ﷺ was mentioned in the presence of Imam Mālik, his skin color would change and he would rock back and forth in such a way that those sitting beside him would be disturbed by it. [165]

163　Ibid 3/131.
164　Ghazālī, *Iḥyā' 'ulūm al-dīn*, K. Ādāb al-samā', al-bāb al-thānī fī āthār al-sam' wa-ādābih.
165　Qāḍī ʿIyāḍ, *al-Shifā* p. 289.

Imam Suyūṭī said: "The lawfulness of standing and dancing during gatherings of *dhikr* and singing has been transmitted from many great imams, including Shaykh al-Islām ʿIzz al-Dīn b. ʿAbd al-Salām (d. 1262)."[166]

Sīdī Aḥmad al-Rifāʿī (d. 1182, may God sanctify his secret) said in his book, "The Authenticated Demonstration," (*al-Burhān al-muʾayyad*) regarding the different forms of ecstasy:

You invoke God in this room, and in doing so you become ecstatic and sway. Jurists whose hearts are veiled say, "The dervishes were dancing," while the knowers of God say, "The dervishes were invoking." He amongst you whose ecstasy is false, whose intention is bad, whose *dhikr* is merely verbal and sullied with ulterior motives, is indeed a mere dancer as the jurists claim. As for the one whose ecstasy is sincere and his intention righteous, he conforms to God's words: **[Those] who listen to the Word, then follow what is most beautiful of it, it is they whom God has guided; it is they who are the possessors of intellect.**[167] He is one of those who, when they **listen to the Word**, seek its meaning. This is what it means to answer the pre-eternal divine call, **"Am I not your Lord?" They said, "Yea, we bear witness."**[168] At that moment, those who heard, heard beyond all boundaries, forms, and attributes. The exquisite savor of this call has become rooted in them through repetition.

166 Suyūṭī, *al-Ḥāwī lil-fatāwī* vol. 2 pp 222-223.
167 Q Zumar 39:18.
168 Q Aʿrāf 7:172.

When God created Adam and made his progeny manifest in the world, that preserved and hidden secret was manifested in them. Thus, when they hear a beautiful melody accompanied with good word, their aspirations fly to the origin where they heard that call. Such are the knowers of God, who were knowers even before the Creation, who love one another in Him, and visit one another for Him, who constantly invoke Him and are totally absorbed and intoxicated by Him.

Such a dervish is called an invoker (*dhākir*), for his spirit dances, his resolve remains sound, his intellect is perfected, and his page is cleared. He took the concealed content from the song, and the secret that was unfolded within him was brought out. For the secret of the song is present within the nature of any person with a spirit who can hear it. Each one hears in the way his nature allows him to, and understands the song in accordance with the limit of his aspiration.

Consider how when a child hears a lullaby, it becomes enraptured and falls asleep, or how when the camel hears the camel-driver's chant, it forgets the weight of its burden and accelerates its steps. This is the intent of the Sufis when they sing and dance, and this gift is not the same as the unlawful type of dance, as some ignorant jurists have claimed. This gift is attained only by the one who masters his own thoughts, and whose heart is protected from Satan's disquieting whispers. [169]

169 Rifāʿī, *al-Burhān al-muʾayyad* pp 52-54.

After the Prophet 🕮, the Companions were certainly the most likely to experience spiritual states during the remembrance of God. It is said that when Sayyidunā 'Umar—and you know well who 'Umar was—heard the verses, **truly thy Lord's Punishment shall come to pass, none can avert it,** [170] he fell into an illness which lasted twenty days.

Let us conclude this explanation of the *ḥaḍra* by quoting from Sīdī Aḥmad Ibn 'Ajība's commentary on Ibn al-Bannā of Saragossa (d. 1321) *al-Mabāḥith al-aṣliyya.* I shall quote the passage in full, for he summarized the matter quite wonderfully, as he always does, may God by pleased with him.

The author [al-Sarqusṭī] said:

Many have delved into sacred music (samā'),
But these folk have therein a meadow.

The Iraqis say it is forbidden,
While the Hijazis permit it.

What he is saying, may God have mercy on him, is that a lot has been said about sacred music (*samā'*), and that some people consider it unlawful while others permit it. As for this group of people, the Sufis, who are in fact God's people, *samā'* is for them a garden and an intoxicating drink coming from a source that they find in their hearts and innermost secrets. This is why

170   Q Ṭūr 52:7-8.

when Imam Junayd was asked about *samā'*, he said: "Anything that unites the heart with God is allowed," or words to that effect.

He then mentioned the disagreement that exists between scholars, in particular the Iraqis, meaning the Ḥanafīs, who declare it unlawful, and Hijazis, meaning the Mālikīs and Shāfi'īs, who declare it lawful or reserve judgment. Abū Muṣ'ab reported that Imam Mālik was asked about *samā'* and answered, "I have never heard anything about it, except that the men of knowledge in our region do not reject it, nor do they avoid it. Only a foolish ignorant, or an Iraqi ascetic with difficult temperament, can reject it."

I [Ibn 'Ajība] say that no intelligent person could deny that *samā'* is lawful in principle, given the hadith about the girls who sang and played a drum in the presence of God's Messenger ﷺ on the day of Eid.

Abū 'Abd al-Raḥmān al-Sulamī (d. 1021) related that 'Ā'isha said: "God's Messenger ﷺ came to my house while my servant girl was singing to me. Then 'Umar came in, and she fled. God's Messenger ﷺ began to laugh. 'Umar asked him why, and he told him. 'Umar said, 'I will not leave until I have heard what God's Messenger ﷺ heard.' So he asked the servant to sing for him, and she did so."

Al-Tujībī reported the same version of the hadith adding that al-Sulamī said, "When Dhū al-Nūn (d. 859) was asked about *samā*, he answered, "It is a genuine inrush (*wārid*) that transports the heart to the Real. He who listens to it with truth will attain realization, while he who listens to it with ego will become a heretic."

Al-Sarī (d. 867) said, "*Samā*ʿ produces rapture in the hearts of the lovers, fear in the hearts of the repenters, and melancholy in the hearts of the yearners."

It has been said that *samā*ʿ is comparable to rain that falls upon dry soil, revitalizing it. Likewise, pure souls bring forth their hidden secrets during *samā*ʿ. Others say that *samā*ʿ stirs the secrets, sorrows, hopes, and yearnings that the heart contains, which may lead a person to weep or become enraptured. Still others say that *samā*ʿ contains a due for every part of the body, so that someone might weep, or cry out, or moan, or dance, or faint. It has also been said that the people of *samā*ʿ are divided into three categories: the repentant, the sincere, and the upright.

Others have said that the people who gather together for *samā*ʿ are divided into three categories: those who listen through their Lord, those who listen through their heart, and those who listen through their ego.

Some say that he who participates in *samā*ʿ needs three characteristics: subtlety, tenderness, and a burning passion, as well as the extinction of his own nature and entrance into the esoteric realities. *Samā*ʿ is only for the one whose selfish interests are annihilated while his rights remain, and whose human nature is extinguished.

He [Ibn al-Bannā] continues: the effect of *samāʿ* depends on the person's inner purity and the strength of the inrush.

Some Shaykhs have said that *samāʿ* is allowed only for those whose heart is alive and whose lower self (*nafs*) is dead. As for he whose lower self is alive and whose heart is dead, it is not allowed for him.

It is said that a saint among the *Abdāl* [lit. the Substitutes] said, "I saw the Prophet ﷺ and asked Him, ''What do you say about the *samāʿ* done by our companions?' He replied, 'It is the purity that is only fulfilled by the greatest knowers of God.'"

Ibn Luyūn al-Tujībī had the final word on this in *al-Ināla*, where he said: "No one could condemn listening to poetry except one ignorant of the Sunna. Ṣāliḥ b. Aḥmad b. Ḥanbal related that he saw his father listening to the singing coming from his neighbor's house." He added, "Anas narrated, 'We were with the Prophet ﷺ when Gabriel came and told Him, "O Messenger of God, the poor of your community will enter heaven five hundred years before the wealthy, which is half a day." He rejoiced at this, and said, "Is there anybody here who can recite a poem to us?" A companion of Badr answered, "Yes, dear Messenger of God." Then he recited:

The snake of passion bit my liver,
And I found for it no doctor or healer,

Excepted the Beloved, with whom I am enraptured;
With him lie my healing and my remedy.

"The Prophet ﷺ became ecstatic at this, as did his Companions, until his cloak fell from his shoulders. When they finished, they all returned to their place, and then Mu'āwiya said, 'What a fine game, O Messenger of God!' He replied, 'No indeed, Mu'āwiya! The one who does not move at the mention of the Beloved is not noble.' Then he divided his cloak into four hundred pieces and gave it to those who were present." Al-Maqdisī and al-Suhrawardī narrated this, and others had much to say about it.

I [Ibn 'Ajība] say that the final verdict on *samā'* is that a distinction must be made: for the folk of esoteric realities (*ahl al-ḥaqā'iq*), there is no doubt that *samā'* is lawful for them, or even recommended as we shall discuss presently. The justification for this is what we have just discussed. As for the folk who follow the outward Law only (*ahl al-sharā'i'*), if there are no women and children present, it is lawful for the repentant, and disliked for others. [171] As for if women and children are present, it should be considered unlawful as a precautionary measure. And God knows best.

The author [Ibn al-Bannā] then alludes to this distinction:

The shaykhs are masters of its arts,
For they made it a pillar of the Path.

---

171 The Dār al-Kutub al-'Ilmiyya edition of Ibn 'Ajība's *al-Futūḥāt al-ilāhiyya* is missing some words in the Arabic. For the full version, see Kattānī's *Mawāhib al-arb* (vol. 2, Dār al-Kutub al-'Ilmiyya, 2016) p. 404.

It is authorized for ascetics,
And recommended for the shaykhs;

But it is almost unlawful for common people,
According to the eminent masters.

I [Ibn ʿAjība] say: He is saying, may God have mercy on him, that the shaykhs find in *samāʿ* different arts, blessings, emotions, states, and inrushes, and this is why they have made it a pillar to which they may resort without relying on it, because it is only an allowance for the weakest, as we shall see, while the strongest have no need of it. As we saw earlier, when Imam Junayd was asked about *samāʿ*, he answered, "Anything that unites the servant with his Lord is allowed."

The final word on the matter is the distinction that the author describes here, which is that *samāʿ* can be permitted (*mubāḥ*), recommended (*mandūb*), or unlawful (*ḥarām*).

Samāʿ is permitted for ascetics because their lower selves are dead to passions and futile pleasures. There is no reason to forbid *samāʿ* for them, nor to recommended it, because they have not yet reached the spiritual degrees of realization (*taḥqīq*) and experiential taste (*dhawq*).

Samāʿ is recommended for the shaykhs and the knowers of God, because it provokes in them ecstasy and inspiration, which extends to the physical realm and envelops the other attendees so that they receive a share of it. For when someone attains realization of a spiritual state, all the present people taste with him part of that state; and anything that leads to spiritual perfection is itself a perfection.

Samāʿ is forbidden for common people, because it generates passions in them, stirs them to commit sins, and awakens in them abject dispositions and base penchants. But if the attendees are not this kind of person, then *samāʿ* is allowed except in the presence of corrupt people, in which case *samāʿ* is totally forbidden in order to prevent what is unlawful. In reality, *samāʿ* is forbidden for common people only because singing is considered a gateway to fornication, and because it creates hypocrisy in the heart.

It has been said that *samāʿ* is melodious wine imbibed by the spirit through the cup of the ear. Each person shall reap what they sow in accordance with their intention. "Zamzam water is for that for which it is drunk," and *samāʿ* is for that for which it is heard.

It has also been said that he who partakes in *samāʿ* with a mind for heresy is a heretic, and he who partakes in *samāʿ* with a mind for spiritual realization will attain it. In matters of love, each will receives what he intends. Someone used to say, "Sing whatever you please, and we shall hear whatever we please." All success is from God. [172]

172 Ibn ʿAjība, *al-Futūḥāt al-ilāhiyya* pp 183-186.

Sīdī Abū Madyan (d. 1198, may God sanctify his secret) said in a poem:

Tell the one who forbids ecstasy to its people,
If you have not tasted the drink of love, then let us be.

While the spirits stir with yearning for the encounter,
The bodies dance. O you who know not the meaning,

Consider the bird imprisoned in its cage,
When it remembers its homeland, it longs to sing,

Freeing what was locked in its heart through its chirping,
And its soul trembles along with its body,

And it dances in its cage, yearning for the meeting;
No sane man could fail to be moved by its song.

So too it is with the spirits of the lovers:
Longing for the higher world causes them
to stir with yearning.

Could we force the bird to remain still
in the midst of its yearning?
Could anyone witness this, and remain unmoved?

✵

The Proper Conduct of *Samāʿ*

Tears are the interpreters of the eye, by which we mean the eye of the heart, the original eye. As for the eyes of the head, they are but a representation of the eye of heart in the physical world. When the eye of the heart is consumed by the fire of passionate love and yearning, the tears of life and love flow from its secret wellspring.

So the sensory world is directly linked to the world of pure meaning; indeed, the sensory world is only one of the expressions and interpreters of the pure meanings. When the heart is touched by total submission and reliance on God, then the body will feel exactly the same thing. Each limb of the body is a pen that writes what is contained in the heart. When the heart softens, the skin trembles. God says: **God has sent down the most beautiful discourse, a Book consimilar, paired, whereat trembles the skin of those who fear their Lord. Then their skin and their hearts soften unto the remembrance of God. That is God's Guidance, wherewith He guides whomsoever He will; and whomsoever God leads astray, no guide has he.** [173]

He also says, **And when they hear that which was sent down unto the Messenger, thou seest their eyes overflow with tears because of the truth they recognize. They say, "Our Lord, we believe, so inscribe us among the witnesses."** [174]

173 Q Zumar 39:23.
174 Q Māʾida 5:83.

Ibn al-Bannā (d. 1321) said:

Speaking is not allowed during samā',
Nor distraction, nor smiling.

Ibn 'Ajība writes in *al-Mabāḥith al-aṣliyya*:

The reason it is not allowed to talk during the *samā'* is that for the knowers of God, the *samā'* is the venue for ecstasy and the pure nectar, and talking distracts the heart, diverts it from the divine presence, and turns it away from the esoteric truth. Therefore it is obligatory to refrain from talking if one wishes to focus one's heart. As for ordinary people, it is allowed because they are close to the level of falsehood anyway, and the slightest thing will return them to it.

Al-Sulamī ﷺ said: "To be still with a present heart and concentrated aspiration, and to listen attentively to what the singers are reciting, is better than joining in with them, because the occasion demands calm and solemnity, and it is good manners on the part of the attendees to listen attentively. **God says: when in its presence they said, "Hearken!"** [175] **He also says: And voices will be humbled before the Compassionate, and you will hear naught but a murmur.**" [176]

As for distraction, it is forbidden because it implies that one's heart is not really in it, and that one has only attended the gathering to provide his soul with entertainment. "Distraction"

---

175 Q Aḥqāf 46:29.
176 Q Ṭā-Hā 20:108.

means to turn to turn away from the *samāʿ* whether with the heart or the body, and become occupied with some other matter. As for smiling during the *samāʿ*, it is discourteous. If someone is overcome with a smile, he should go outside for a moment. Otherwise, he should be escorted out [of the gathering] and rebuked.

Al-Sulamī added, "Anyone who is given to smiling and distraction should not attend gatherings of *samāʿ*."

It is said that Shaykh Abū ʿAbd Allāh b. Khafīf (d. 982) said, "I once attended a gathering of *samāʿ* in Bushrān in the company of my Shaykh, Aḥmad b. Yaḥyā. It so happened that there were some other people in the area also holding a gathering. My Shaykh very much enjoyed the gathering and began to turn in ecstasy, and one of the worldly people in the crowd nearby smiled. The Shaykh took a large lamp and threw it at him [or at the wall], and three of the lamp's feet became lodged in the wall and stuck fast. He was a righteous man who for thirty years had stayed up all night long in prayer and devotion." [177]

The Moaning of the Palm Trunk

In *al-Shifā*, Qāḍī ʿIyāḍ relates the hadith of the palm trunk in which the Companions described how it moaned with love and

---

177   Ibn ʿAjība, *al-Futūḥāt al-ilāhiyya* pp 190-191.

yearning for God's Messenger ﷺ. Jābir b. ʿAbd Allāh said, "The mosque was built with palm trunks with a roof laid on top of them. When the Prophet ﷺ addressed the people, he would lean against one of the trunks. When the pulpit was built for him, we heard that trunk make a sound like the moan of a camel."

The narration of Anas has: "Until the mosque was shaken by its moaning." Sahl's narration has, "People wept a great deal when they witnessed this." The narrations of al-Muṭṭalib and Ubayy have, "It nearly split and burst apart, until the Prophet ﷺ came to it and placed his hand on it. Then it fell still. The Prophet ﷺ said, "It is weeping at the remembrance it has lost."

Another added, "By the One in Whose hand is my soul, if I had not attended to it, it would have remained moaning like that until the Day of Resurrection, out of grief for God's Messenger."

God's Messenger ﷺ commanded that it be buried beneath the pulpit, according to the hadiths of al-Muṭṭalib, Sahl b. Saʿd, and Isḥāq on the authority of Anas. One of the transmissions from Sahl says, "It was buried under his pulpit, or placed on the roof." The hadith of Ubayy adds, "so that when the Prophet ﷺ prayed, it would be in front of him. When the mosque was demolished, Ubayy took it and it remained in his possession until the earth consumed it and it returned to dust."

Al-Isfirāʾinī said, "The Prophet ﷺ called it to him, and it came furrowing through the earth and clung to him. Then he commanded it and it returned to its place." In the hadith of Burayda, the Prophet said, "If you like, I will put you back in the orchard where you were, so your roots can grow and your creation can be completed, and you will have fruit and leaves again. Or, if you like, I will plant you in the Garden of Paradise, so that the friends of God can eat from your fruit." The prophet listened to hear what it would say. It said, "Plant me in Paradise so that the friends of God can eat my fruit, and I will be in a place where I will never decay." Those who were near it heard what it said. The Prophet ﷺ said, "So be it." Then he said, "It has chosen the Lasting Abode over the Passing Abode."

When al-Ḥasan b. ʿAli told this story, he wept and said, "Servants of God, the wood moaned with yearning for God's Messenger ﷺ because of his position. You are the ones who should yearn to meet him!" [178]

A poet said:

The trunk moaned with longing for you,
And shed tears of lament for you;

It wept and sobbed
At the loss of your words and your touch.

How then could my heart not moan for you,
How could not my dream not be to catch your gaze,

---

178 Qāḍī ʿIyāḍ, *al-Shifā* p. 307.

And to meet you on the promised Day,
And behold your blessed face?

I would sacrifice my kin and possessions for you,
And give my soul for eternity,

I would be joyful and blissful forever
If I could give my life to please you.

Beloved of my heart, pardon me, do not blame me,
That my love cannot compare to your worth;

My sins pin me down, prevent my ascension,
Though I long to rise to your heights.

Perhaps my love will elevate my spirit,
And mend the flaws of its passion for you.

3.

The Patched Cloak (*al-muraqqaʿa*)

In the Arabic language:

Raqqaʿa al-thawb means "to patch a garment." [179] A *muraqqaʿa*, plural *muraqqaʿāt*, means a garment patched together from could be wool, fur or leather. [180]

In the Terminology of the Karkariya Order:

The patched cloak is an expression of self-concealment in the garb of the Essence's beauty. This divine beauty, which remains non-manifest in the differentiation of the Names, discloses itself in the colors of the Higher Bow. [181] The patched cloak is a

---

179 *Al-Muʿjam al-ʿarabī al-asāsī* p. 542.

180 Ibn ʿAjība, *al-Futūḥāt al-ilāhiyya* p. 130.

181 Translator's note: In the Shaykh's teachings, the higher bow (*al-qaws al-ʿulwī*) contrasts with the lower bow (*al-qaws al-suflī*) of the letter Bā'. Whereas the lower bow is visible and represents the revealed Law, the higher bow is invisible and represents esoteric realities. Together, the two dimensions of religion form a complete circle whose center is the dot (*nuqṭa*). This central dot is the secret of the Qur'ān with which ʿAlī ibn Abī Ṭālib identifies himself in the statement, "I am the secret of the dot." In the definition of the patched cloak above, the colors of the "upper bow" also suggest the rainbow.

declaration of the soul's allegiance to the Spirit for the purpose of entering upon and ascending through its levels.

The *muraqqaʿa* in the Holy Qur'ān:

God says: **Thus he lured them on through deception. And when they tasted of the tree, their nakedness was exposed to them, and they began to sew together the leaves of the Garden to cover themselves. And their Lord called out to them, "Did I not forbid you from that tree, and tell you that Satan is a manifest enemy unto you?"** [182]

God says: **O Children of Adam! We have indeed sent down upon you raiment to cover your nakedness, and rich adornment. But the raiment of reverence, that is better. This is among the signs of God, that haply they may remember.** [183]

God says: **O Children of Adam! Let not Satan tempt you, as he caused your parents to go forth from the Garden, stripping them of their raiment to show them their nakedness. Surely he sees you—he and his tribe—whence you see them not. We have indeed made the satans the friends of those who do not believe.** [184]

God says: **God sets forth a parable: a town secure and at peace, its provision coming unto it abundantly from every side.**

---

182 Q Aʿrāf 7:22.
183 Q Aʿrāf 7:26.
184 Q Aʿrāf 7:27.

Yet, it was ungrateful for the blessings of God; so God let it taste the garment of hunger and fear for that which they had wrought. [185]

God says: Truly God will cause those who believe and perform righteous deeds to enter Gardens with rivers running below, adorned therein with bracelets of gold and pearl, and therein their clothes will be of silk. [186]

God says: And He it is Who made the night a garment for you, and made sleep repose, and made day a resurrection. [187]

God says: [Did We not] make the night a garment? [188]

The *muraqqa'a* in the noble Sunna:

Abū Burda said, "'Ā'isha brought out to us a patched woolen garment, and said: "The spirit of God's Messenger ﷺ was taken away while he was wearing this." Another narration states that Abū Burda said, "Aisha brought out to us a thick waist-wrapper like the ones made by the Yemenites, and also a garment of the type called *mulabbada*." [189]

Ibn Kaysān narrated that Abū Umāma related that God's Messenger ﷺ said, "*Badhādha* is part of faith", three times. Abū Umāma's son 'Abd Allāh asked him, "What is *badhādha*?" He replied, "To dress modestly." [190]

---

185   Q Naḥl 16:112.
186   Q Ḥajj 22:23.
187   Q Furqān 25:47.
188   Q Naba' 78:10.
189   Bukhārī, *Ṣaḥīḥ* #2894.
190   Aḥmad, *Zuhd*, #29.

Sahl b, Mu'ādh related on the authority of his father that God's Messenger ﷺ said, "When someone holds back his anger though he could take vengeance if he wanted to, God Almighty will summon him before all of mankind and let him choose whichever maiden of Paradise he desires. And when someone refrains from wearing fancy clothes, though he can afford them, out of humility before God, God Almighty will summon him before all of mankind and let him choose whichever cloak of faith he desires." [191]

Umm Khālid bint Khālid related that the Prophet ﷺ was given some clothes including a black dress. He said, "To whom shall we give this dress to wear?" The people kept silent, whereupon he said, "Fetch Umm Khālid." They fetched her, and the Prophet ﷺ put the dress on her and said, "May you live so long that your dress will wear out, and you will mend it many times." The dress was pattered with markings of green, yellow and red, which the Prophet ﷺ showed to Umm Khālid, saying, "This is *sanā*", which means "beauty" in the Abyssinian language. [192]

It was narrated from Mu'ādh b. Jabal that God's Messenger ﷺ said, "Shall I not tell you about the kings of Paradise?" I said, "Indeed, do." He said, "A weak and oppressed man who wears tattered clothes and is not paid any heed. If he swears an oath by God, God fulfills it." [193]

---

191 Aḥmad, *Musnad* #15312.
192 Bukhārī, *Ṣaḥīḥ* #5425, #5403; Ḥākim, *Mustadrak* #7471, #2304.
193 Ibn Mājah, *Sunan* #4113.

✪

The Basis of the *Muraqqaʿa*

It is the tradition of the righteous, the hallmark of the pious, and the clothing of the gnostics. It is the distinctive sign of the sincere disciple who is in his search for the Real, extinguished in the love of his Shaykh, and divested of his own will.

The patched robe is the symbol of deferential resignation, entrustment, and putting oneself in the hands of the perfected gnostic shaykh. In this way, the shaykh will allow the disciple to see the flaws of his soul and its levels, so that it is purified and elevated from the *nafs ammāra* (the evil-enjoining soul), to the *nafs lawwāma* (lamenting soul), to the *nafs muṭma'inna* (the soul at peace), to the *nafs rāḍiya* (the content soul), to the *nafs marḍiyya* (the contenting soul), and finally to the *nafs rājiʿa ilā rabbihā* (the soul returned unto its Lord).

It has been said that the one who never sees a successful person will never succeed, and the one who has no Shaykh has Iblīs for his shaykh. What do you think about the one who learns a craft without a teacher?

In general, a tree that grows by itself does not give edible fruits; and even if it does, those fruits never reach the same quality as those of a tended orchard.

Abū Hurayra narrated that the Prophet ﷺ said, "Faith has seventy-some (or sixty-some) branches, the foremost of which is to say, 'There is no god but God', and the least of which is to remove harmful objects from the road. Modesty is a branch of faith." [194]

So the least branch of faith is removing harmful objects from the road to God, and nothing is more harmful than your soul. It is your greatest enemy, so strive to remove its harm, and know that there is nothing harder for the soul than the loss of people's esteem. This is reason the *muraqqaʿa* is one of the founding principles of the disciple's spiritual education in our blessed Order.

God says: **O thou who art covered, arise and warn! Thy Lord magnify! Thy garments purify!** [195]

God has a **garment** in which he dresses his servant when his love is genuine. This clothing helps the disciple to detach from the garb of the herebelow, and to suffice with a *muraqqaʿa* or a simple robe which he wears here and there without worrying about other people. This disciple no longer sees other than his Lord, and prefers the eternal to the ephemeral.

Abū Hurayra narrated that God's Messenger ﷺ said, "O people! God is Pure and accepts only that which is pure. God has commanded the believers as He has commanded His messengers by saying: **O messengers! Eat of the good things and**

---

194 Muslim, *Ṣaḥīḥ* #54.
195 Q Muddaththir, 74:1-4.

work righteousness. [196] And He says, **O you who believe! Eat of the good things We have provided you.**" [197] Then he made mention of a man who travels for a long period of time, disheveled and covered with dust. He lifts his hand towards the sky and cries, "My Lord! My Lord!" But his food is unlawful, his drink unlawful, his clothes unlawful, and his nourishment unlawful. How, then can his prayer be answered?" [198]

How could your prayers be answered while your clothes are unlawful? The evil of your deeds is manifested in your outward appearance. The angels never enter a house where a dog lives, so how could the Lights of the Real flow through you, while your body is clothed in the unlawful? Remove all your clothes, and put on the clothing of piety!

God says: **And He it is Who made the night a garment for you, and made sleep repose, and made day a resurrection.** [199]

The dark **night** of your soul is the primordial **garment** of all, which God made as a veil between His creation and the secrets of pre-eternity. He who is predestined for the divine love will be guided to a lordly Shaykh who knows God, and who will **resurrect** the **day** of his spirit, thereby covering the sign of the **night** with the sign of the **day**. Moreover, **the sign of the day is sight-giving,** [200] and so he will **see** the secrets that God has folded within him. When he gains strength and mastery, his

196 Q Muʾminūn 23:51.
197 Q Baqara 2:172.
198 Muslim, *Ṣaḥīḥ* #1692.
199 Q Furqān 25:47.
200 Q Isrāʾ 17:11.

inner being will imprint over his outer being; for the outer is only the reflection of the inner, and a man is clothed in nothing other than his inmost secret.

God's Messenger ﷺ said, "Keep whatever secret you wish; for by God, whenever any man or woman keeps a secret, God clothes them in its robe. If it is good, then it will be good; and if it is bad, then it will be bad. Even if one you accomplished a good deed behind seventy veils, God would make it visible so that people spoke well of him. And even if one of you hid something evil behind seventy veils, God would make it visible so that people spoke ill of him." [201]

✿

Benefits of the *Muraqqaʻa*

The *muraqqaʻa* has many benefits in this world and the hereafter, which Imam Ibn al-Bannā of Saragossa (d. 1321) ﷺ enumerated in *al-Mabāḥith al-aṣliyya*, on which Ibn ʻAjība commentated comprehensively, as follows:

[The author Ibn al-Bannā says:]

The Sufis choose the muraqqaʻa
Because of the characteristics we will mention:

---

201 Abū Nuʻaym, *Ḥilya* #6355.

This first: it dispels pride;
It protects against cold and heat;

It costs little to obtain;
Worldly people do not covet it;

It debases the soul, and extends the life;
It cultivates patience, following ‘Umar's example;

The one who wears it appears fearful,
Which inspires him to be humble.

[Ibn ‘Ajība comments:] The *muraqqa‘a* is a garment patched together from many kinds of material, whether colored or not, which could be wool, fur or leather. The Sufis prefer it to other kinds of clothing for ten reasons:

The first reason is that it dispels and excludes pride, and it cultivates humility—unless the intention of the one who wears it is to try to show himself as a pious man, in which case it is unlawful to wear it. Likewise, if he wears it to distinguish himself from the dervishes who do not wear it, or if he thinks that wearing it makes him better than others, then the obtained effect is the opposite of the desired effect.

The second reason is that it is composed in such a way that it protects from heat because of how the pieces of fabric are stitched together. It also protects from cold because of the fabric's thickness.

The third reason is that it is very cheap, because it is made from fabrics that were destined for the garbage heap and would cost nothing to give away. However, if someone chooses fabrics of good quality for it, then the *muraqqaʿa* loses its true purpose and no longer gives its fruits, becoming just like any other garment.

The fourth reason is that the patched cloak in itself is not coveted by thieves or others. However, its honorable status is recognized, and if a dervish were to pull the cloak away from plundering thieves, they would pay no regard to it after inquiring him about it. Instead the thieves would return the cloak back to him and ask forgiveness for offending him. This is something that is well-known to have occurred. Wearing the *muraqqaʿa* in order to be respected is thus permitted, according to Shaykh Aḥmad Zarrūq ﷺ.

The fifth reason is that wearing the *muraqqaʿa* wards off many evil things because of the respect people have for the one who wears it, as they recognize him as a righteous person. This is permitted if the intention is to ward off harm, not to attract benefit, in accordance with the verse: **O Prophet! Tell thy wives and thy daughters, and the women of the believers to draw their cloaks (*jalābīb*) over themselves. Thus is it likelier that they will be known and not be disturbed. And God is Forgiving, Merciful.** [202] This is implied by Ibn al-Bannā's words, "Worldly people do not covet it."

---

202   Q Aḥzāb 33:59.

The sixth reason is that it encourages self-abasement among one's fellow men, which causes the soul's death, wherein is its life. In this sense, al-Shushtarī (d. 1269) said, speaking on behalf of the Real:

If you desire union with us, then your death is a condition;
The one in whom trace residues remain does not attain union.

In the debasement of the soul, there is also the loss of rank and dignity, which is a condition for realizing the station of sincerity. It also leads to obscurity and the loss of reputation (*khumūl*), which brings peace and repose, for such a person will not be known for anything other than what he is, nor is he perceived as being informed about important affairs. If he is absent, no one notices it; if he is present, his opinion is not sought. In this sense, the Prophet ﷺ said, "Many a man there is whose face is dusty, his hair unkempt, his clothes tattered, and no one pays attention to him. Yet if he were too swear an oath by God, God would fulfill it."

The seventh reason is that it lifts one's saintly aspiration and diminishes the concern that one has for the opinion of others. After all, the admiration of admirers brings nothing but spiritual harm, and the one who wears the *muraqqaʿa* no longer pays attention to others. Both admirers and critics are equal for him.

A shaykh once said to a young man, "Beware of this *muraqqaʿa*! People honor you because of it." The young man replied: "They only honor us for God's sake." The shaykh said, "How good it is to be honored for God's sake!"

The eighth reason is that it has been said that wearing the *muraqqaʿa* extends a person's life; this is because of the blessings the *muraqqaʿa* brings to the one who wears it, in the sense that in a short period of time, the one who wears the *muraqqaʿa* attains things that would take years for a person who does not wear it to attain.

In this sense, Sayyidunā Ibn ʿAṭāʾ Allāh al-Iskandarī said in his *Ḥikam*: "Whoever is blessed in his life-span is able to attain, in a short time, things that are incomparable and indescribable. The worship of the knowers of God is multiplied over and over." He also said in his *Ḥikam*: "No deed arising from an ascetic heart is small, and no deed arising from an avaricious heart is large."

It has also been said that the *muraqqaʿa* literally increases one's lifespan, for it contains a special kind of blessing, and that wearing the *muraqqaʿa* foretells a long life. God knows best.

The ninth reason is that it cultivates patience and self-restraint, the merits of which are known to all. God says: **Surely those who are patient shall be paid their reward in full without reckoning;** [203] and He says, **give glad tidings to the patient;** [204] and, **Truly God is with the patient.** [205]

---

203 Q Zumar 39:10.
204 Q Baqara 2:155.
205 Q Baqara 2:153.

One of the Companions said, "Patience to religion is as the head to the body, and patience is the foundation of religious leadership and pious adherence." God says: **We appointed leaders from among them who guided by Our Command when they were patient and had sure faith in Our signs.** [206]

Wearing the *muraqqaʿa* also protects against major sins, because it makes its wearer feel too ashamed to stray anywhere near them. So the *muraqqaʿa* is a protection against grave sin, and the patience needed to wear it is equivalent, as it were, to the patience needed to confront all sinful things.

The tenth reason is that wearing the *muraqqaʿa* is following the example of the Commander of the Faithful, Sayyidunā ʿUmar b. al-Khaṭṭāb ﷺ. God's Messenger ﷺ said, "Follow those who come after me: Abū Bakr and ʿUmar." So following them is obeying the instructions of the Prophet ﷺ.

The one who wears the *muraqqaʿa* also encapsulates all the reasons that led ʿUmar ﷺ to wear it. ʿUmar wore a *muraqqaʿa* with thirteen patches between the shoulders, one of which was made of leather. When he swapped it for another garment on the day of the conquest of Jerusalem, following the advice of the Muslims, he exclaimed, "I do not recognize myself," and put his *muraqqaʿa* back on.

So it was ʿUmar's personal choice to wear the *muraqqaʿa* for the sake of humility, not out of necessity, for he was not short of wealth either before or after he became Caliph. [207]

206 Q Sajda 32:24.
207 Ibn ʿAjība, *al-Futūḥāt al-ilāhiyya* pp 130-132.

✿

The *Muraqqaʿa* of Sayyidunā ʿUmar ﷺ

Sayyidunā ʿUmar ibn al-Khaṭṭāb did not conquer Jerusalem, the city of the Ascension, in the midst of a great army of powerful men and horses. On the contrary, he crossed deserts and wastelands wearing his *muraqqaʿa*, accompanied by a servant and their modest mount, reciting Sūrah Yā-Sīn as they went. Sometimes ʿUmar would ride the animal, and sometimes it was the turn of his servant, and other times they would let the animal have a rest. With this journey, al-Fārūq provided a lesson for all mindful people to contemplate.

When he reached the camp of the Muslim army, Abū ʿUbayda and the other Companions gave ʿUmar a welcome fit for the Commander of the Faithful. Then Abū ʿUbayda leaned to kiss ʿUmar's hand, and ʿUmar in turn bent down to kiss Abū ʿUbayda's feet. This is how the Companions greeted one another, having been educated in the school of the Beloved ﷺ— yet there are those who condemn us for kissing one another's hands!

The companions encouraged ʿUmar to ride another mount and to wear appropriate clothing for the greatness of the day, and they kept at him until finally he accepted. He was presented with a mighty horse. When he mounted it, it began to strut around. He immediately dismounted saying, "Until this day, I did not know that the demons could be ridden! I must take back my *muraqqaʿa* and my mount."

Then he headed for the holy city, and while he was walking, he waded through the mud of a stream near Jerusalem. He took off his shoes and held them in one hand while the other hand was holding the bridle of his mount. Abū ‘Ubayda said to him, "Commander of the Faithful, do you mean to wade through the mud barefoot while wearing that *muraqqa‘a*? These people are princes and kings, who set great store in appearances." ‘Umar hit him on his chest and said, "If anyone other than you had said this, ‘Abū ‘Ubayda, I would have hit his head with this whip. Verily, we were the lowliest and most disgraced of all people, and then God honored us with Islam. If we seek honor from other than Islam, God will disgrace us once more."

May God be pleased with ‘Umar, the great Discerner (*Fārūq*) of Islam! Indeed, there is no honor to be found in ephemeral shells; all that matters is a sound heart extinguished in the divine presence. So it was that ‘Umar arrived, covered in mud, holding in his hand the bridle of his mount as his servant rode it, his feet covered in mud. As soon as the clerics of Jerusalem saw him approaching, they said: "By God, he is the one!" After the siege that had gone on for four months, they gave him the keys to the city without the least resistance. Their leader, the Patriarch, brought the keys to him. After greeting the Caliph, he said to him, "He who will receive the keys to Jerusalem must have three characteristics. First, he will come walking while his servant will be riding. Second, he will come with his feet covered in mud. As for the third, let me count the number of patches on your garment." He counted seventeen patches (or some narrations say fourteen or twelve), and said, "Here is the third." Then he gave the keys of Jerusalem to the Commander of the Faithful.

The question is not to wear beautiful clothing and to say, "Here I am!" Wear what you like, but never forget that the clerics of Jerusalem gave the keys to the city to a noble man wearing a *muraqqaʿa*.

✧

The Symbolism of Colors in the Qurʾān

God says: **When Moses sought water for his people, We said, "Strike the rock with thy staff." Then twelve springs gushed forth from it; each people knew their drinking place.** [208]

The One Who made springs of water gush forth from the stone was obviously able to provide the Israelites with water without any secondary causes. But God is teaching us His cosmic order, which is that things are done through means and causes. He is also teaching us not to judge based on outward appearances, for the one who judges others on the basis of appearances rarely hits the mark.

The staff of Moses symbolizes the *Alif* of *tawḥīd*. The *Alif* of the Name of Majesty, *Allāh*, is the secret of the cosmos and the secret of the unification of unification (*jamʿ al-jamʿ*). The *Alif*

___

208   Q Baqara 2:60.

flows in all letters, and the person who attains realization of the motto of sincerity, "there is no god but God," will find that it is composed of none other than an *Alif*.

For the people of spiritual realization, the *Alif* is not a letter, but rather all the letters are manifestations and disclosures of the *Alif*. It flows in all letters just as number one flows in all numbers.

So Moses struck the heart with the *Alif* of *tawḥīd* upon the stone of the *Hā'*, and the twelve letters of *tawḥīd* gushed forth from it: *lā ilāha illā Allāh*, each letter symbolizing one of God's springs; and each people knew their drinking place. Some people drank from the spring of the Essence, others from the spring of the Attributes; some from union, others from separation; some from rigor, others from ease; some from extinction, others from subsistence—each in accordance with what was destined for them upon the Tablet of Eternity. Twelve springs with twelve colors: this is the secret of the diversity of manifestation-sites in the cosmos through the *Hā'* of the divine Name.

The letter *Hā'* of the Name *Allāh*, which is visible in this ephemeral cosmos, represented with the presences of colors.

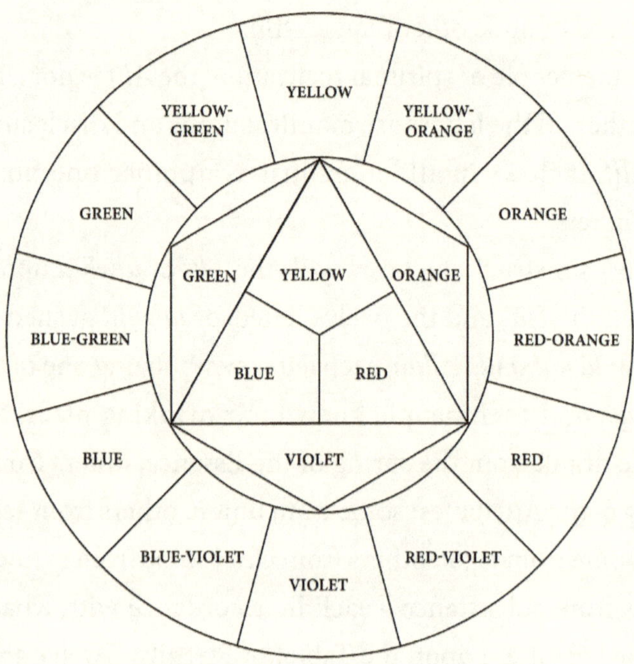

Divine wisdom ensures that this universe has harmonious correspondences with the beauty that is inherent to man. As such, every color traces back to these twelve colors, just as all the knowledge of this cosmos has its source in the twelve letters of *tawḥīd*.

In God's book, the colors bear deep significance, and play a key role in the Qur'ānic expression, both figuratively and literally.

God says: **Hast thou not considered that God sends down water from the sky, wherewith We bring forth fruits of diverse**

colors? And in the mountains are streaks of white and red, of diverse hues, and others pitch-black. [209]

Dear disciple, you are like earth, inert and still, containing everything on its inside and nothing on the surface. But when the water of divine inspiration falls, the earth trembles and produces shoots of knowledge of every color.

The sincere disciple who truly desires God's Face is like the soil, and the shaykh is like the rainwater. When the water falls upon the disciple's soil, the earth of his body gives forth the twelve colors of the patched cloak (*muraqqaʿa*).

Abū Mūsā reported that the Prophet ﷺ said: "The guidance and knowledge with which God has sent me is like rain that falls on land. The fertile part of the land absorbs the water and brings forth much grass and herbs. Another part which is solid holds back the water, and God benefits people with it so that they may drink, water their animals, and irrigate. But then some of it falls into an abyss, which neither retains the water nor produces plants. Such is the likeness of the one who understands the religion of God and benefits from that with which God has sent me; he learns and teaches others. Then there is the one who neither raises his head to it, nor accepts God's guidance with which I have been sent." [210]

In this sense, Sīdī Abū Madyan al-Ghawth (may God sanctify his secret) said in one of his poems:

209　Q Fāṭir 35:27.
210　Bukhārī, *Ṣaḥīḥ* #78.

Every land on which you alight is revived by you,
As if you were rain that falls upon the land.

Colors have a clear symbolic significance in the Qur'ān. The color can refer to power, mercy, or to divine beauty. It can symbolize life or death, unbelief or faith, guidance or error. But these are abstract concepts; they can only be touched or seen through a descent of color which clarifies their reality and meaning. This descent is like the descent of knowledge in milk.

The diversity and mixture of colors is a form of beauty that pleases the eye, enraptures the heart, and invigorates the spirit. In this way, God links the diversity of colors to meditation and contemplation: **And among His signs are the creation of the heavens and the earth and the variation in your tongues and colors. Truly in that are signs for those who know.** [211] So diversity is one of the signs of God, and He made diversity of color a reminder for those who have intelligence.

Have you ever studied a rose, and contemplated the harmonious arrangement of its colors? Have you delved into its deep meanings, and noticed the subtleties of its beauty? God says: **The sky shall be rent asunder, and become a crimson rose (warda).** [212] Observe how God compares the sundering of the heavens to the opening of a rose when it spreads its petals. Taste the meanings of the Qur'ān, for there is nothing sweeter than the words of our Lord.

211 Q Rūm 30:22.
212 Q Raḥmān 55:37.

So the diversity of colors is a Qur'ānic reality that affirms the harmony between mankind and the cosmos. God created the fruits with different colors: **Hast thou not considered that God sends down water from the sky, wherewith We bring forth fruits of diverse colors?** [213]

He also diversified the colors of animals: **"And of mankind, beasts, and cattle there are, likewise, those of diverse colors. [Yet] only those among His servants who know fear God. Truly God is Mighty, Forgiving.** [214]

He diversified the colors of the drink that comes from the bellies of bees: **A drink of diverse hues comes forth from their bellies wherein there is healing for mankind. Truly in that is a sign for a people who reflect.** [215] Indeed, God's Messenger ﷺ compared the believer to the bee: "The believer is like a bee, which eats only that which is good, and produces only that which is good." [216]

Why, then, do you not bring out your inward spiritual realities with all their varied secrets and colors, and then adorn yourself with them outwardly?

God created and embellished the entire universe with varied colors in order to make life more enjoyable and tranquil. Then He gathered everything and folded it within you, because you are the goal, not the universe.

---

213 Q Fāṭir 35:27.
214 Q Fāṭir 35:28.
215 Q Naḥl 16:69.
216 Ibn Ḥibbān, *Ṣaḥīḥ* #250.

In this sense, it has been said:

You think yourself an insignificant object,
Though the greater world is contained within you.

To wear the colored *muraqqaʿa* is to adorn oneself outwardly with the hidden worlds that the Lord of the Worlds placed within His vicegerent. It is a message of love for all God's creatures; for in our *zāwiya*, our way is the way of love, and our school is the school of passion.

I follow the religion of love wherever it heads;
Love is my religion and my faith.

✿

The Garment of Reverence (*libās al-taqwā*)

O Children of Adam! We have indeed sent down upon you garments to cover your nakedness, and rich adornment. But the garment of reverence, that is better. This is among the signs of God, that haply they may remember. [217]

Imam Rūzbihān Baqlī (d. 1209) said in his *Tafsīr*:

Each group has its own garment. The gnostics wear the garment of gnosis; the lovers wear the **garment** of love; the yearn-

---

217 Q Aʿrāf 7:26.

ers wear the **garment** of yearning; the monotheists wear the **garment** of monotheism; the renunciants wear the **garment** of renunciation; the reverent wear the **garment of reverence**; the saints wear the **garment** of sainthood; the prophets wear the **garment** of prophethood; the messengers wear the **garment** of messengerhood. Moreover, each **garment** has an outer part and an inner part. The inner part is made beautiful for God's eyes, while the outer part is made beautiful for the eyes of the revealed Law.

Each person has a selfish interest in each garment, but there is not selfish interest in the **garment of reverence**. These **garments** are clothing for common people, whereas the God's **garment** is for those who are extinguished in God and characterized by His attributes. All **garments** are naught compared to God's **garment**.

Thus, God's Messenger ﷺ referred to his own station of adornment with God's attributes and Lights by saying, "He who sees me, sees the Real (*al-Ḥaqq*)."

The words **to cover your nakedness** mean that you are all divested of the Lights of eternity, and that the nakedness of temporality have exposed upon you. Therefore you must cover the nakedness of temporality with the **garment** of eternity, and the nakedness of ignorance with the **garment** of knowledge, and the nakedness of servanthood with the **garment** of lordship.

Imam al-Wāsiṭī (d. 932) said that the word *saw'a*, "**nakedness**", means "ignorance." The most beautiful adornment is for the servant to don the **garment of reverence**, for it is a shield that cannot be breached by the plots of the envious. **Reverence** is the clothing of the heart, and its sign is pious fear. Reverence is courtesy with God, which means to no longer see other than Him.

Someone said that the **garment** of guidance is for common people, while the **garment of reverence** is for the advanced seekers; the **garment** of divine awe (*hayba*) is for the gnostics, while the **garment** of splendor is for the worldly; the **garment** of the encounter and witnessing is for the saints, and the **garment** of the Presence is for the prophets.

The Master [al-Qushayrī, d. 1072)] said, "The clothing of the heart is the **garment of reverence**. It indicates the sincerity of the person's intention through the total abandonment of all worldly desires. The clothing of the spirit is a **garment of sanctity** (*taqdīs*); it consists of forsaking worldly ties and removing obstacles. The clothing of the innermost secret (*sirr*) is made of reverence; it means to negate all familiar comforts (*musākanāt*) and rid oneself of diversions (*mulāḥāẓāt*).[218]

Choose the **garment** you would like to wear in accordance with the degree of your saintly aspiration, your love, and your proximity to the Real. Beware of paying attention to the average believer, for it is a hopeless task to seek people's approval. Choose what is lasting over what is destined to pass away. Choose the real over the unreal.

---

218 Baqlī, *'Arā'is al-bayān* vol. 1 pp 427-428.

The *muraqqaʿa* is the heritage of our father Adam, and the origin of all clothing. It is the first clothing man ever wore.

Sīdī Ibn ʿAjība, may God sanctify his secret, said in his commentary on the verse, **they began to sew together the leaves of the Garden to cover themselves,** [219] "They patched the leaves on top of each other to cover themselves. It is said that the leaves were from a fig tree. Thus Adam was the first man to wear the *muraqqaʿa*." [220]

The patched cloak removes the one who wears it away from places and things that incur the Lord's wrath. It is like a therapeutic treatment that prevents the one who wears it from entering spaces of diversion and heedlessness, and engaging in frivolous talk.

The *muraqqaʿa* is the emblem of sound orientation. ʿAbd Allāh b. Sarjas al-Muzanī narrated that the Prophet ﷺ said, "Sound orientation, deliberation, and moderation are one twenty-fourth of prophethood." [221]

The term "sound orientation" (*samt*) can have a lot of meanings. One of those meanings is that you have the bearing and comportment of the people of goodness and righteousness. What a great honor to serve one of the parts of prophethood, to be linked to one part of the blessed words of *tawḥīd*, and to be affiliated with one letter of *lā ilāha illā Allāh, Muḥammad rasūl Allāh*—isn't that composed of twenty-four letters?

219 Q Aʿrāf 7:22.
220 Ibn ʿAjība, *al-Baḥr al-madīd* vol. 2 p. 345.
221 Tirmidhī, *Jāmiʿ* #1930.

God's Messenger ﷺ wore all the colors, so gather the Sunna of the Beloved within yourself. If you long for his companionship, he will only come to you through your soul, so stand up and walk towards him. Stop dithering!

Ibn 'Aṭāʾ Allāh al-Iskandarī (may God sanctify his secret) said in one of his aphorisms: "If you were to be united with Him only after the extinction of your vices and the effacement of your pretensions, you would never be united with Him. Instead, when He wants to unite you to Himself, He covers your attribute with His attribute, and hides your quality with His quality. Thus He unites you to Himself by virtue of what comes from Him to you, not by virtue of what goes from you to Him."[222]

So cover your attributes with His attributes, your ignorance with His knowledge, your debasement with His might, your non-existence with His existence, your darkness with the Lights of His attributes, manifested through the colors of the presences disclosed in the *muraqqaʿa*. In this way, you will attain His proximity and reach His contentment.

222 See Danner's translation of *The Book of Wisdom*, aphorism #130, p. 79.

✦

The Story of Sayyidunā Uways al-Qaranī (d. 657)

In the *Ḥilya*, Abū Nuʿaym relates the story of one of the greatest Followers, Sayyidunā Uways al Qaranī when he met al-Fārūq and Sayyidunā ʿAlī. Uways used to wear clothes made of discarded patches of fabric. He was totally unknown to the people of the earth, but known to the people of heaven. Why are some people against wearing the *muraqqaʿa*, when Sayyidunā Uways and Sayyidunā ʿUmar b. al-Khaṭṭāb wore it?

Abū Hurayra related that God's Messenger ﷺ was with a group of Companions when he said: "Tomorrow, a man of Paradise will pray with us." Abū Hurayra said: "I hoped I was this man, so I went the next day to the mosque, and prayed behind the Prophet ﷺ, and stayed until everybody had left. Then a black man came in wearing a waist-wrapper made of a patched ragged cloth. He approached and put his hand into the hand of God's Messenger ﷺ, then said: 'Prophet of God, pray to God for me.' The Prophet ﷺ prayed that he be granted martyrdom. A strong scent of musk emanated from him. I asked, 'O Messenger of God, is he the man?' He answered, 'Yes, he is. He is a slave of such-and-such tribe.' I said: 'Won't you buy him to set him free, Prophet of God?' He replied, 'And why would I do that, when God wants to make him one of the kings of Paradise, Abū Hurayra? Indeed, there are kings and lords for the people of Paradise, and this black man has become one of them. Abū

Hurayra, God loves in His creation the reverent pure ones who are hidden and innocent, whose faces are dusty, whose hair is unkempt, whose stomachs are empty of aught but lawful food. When they ask for audiences with rulers, they are not admitted. When they request gentlewomen's hands in marriage, they are refused. When they are absent, they are not missed; and when they are present, they are not noticed. When they are successful, no one rejoices. When they fall sick, no one visits them. And when they die, no one attends their funerals.'

"The Companions asked him, 'Messenger of God, how are we to recognize such a man?" He ﷺ replied, 'Uways al-Qaranī is one such.' They asked him: 'And who is Uways al-Qaranī?' He ﷺ replied, 'He has bluish-black eyes. His shoulders are broad. He is of medium height. He has dark skin. His chin touches his chest as he stares at the ground on which he prostrates. His right hand is on his left hand. He recites the Qur'ān and weeps for his soul. He wears two tattered garments. No one notices him. He wears a woolen waist-wrapper and a woolen shawl. He is unknown to the people of earth, but known to the people of heaven. If He swore an oath by God, God would fulfill his oath. There is a white mark under his left shoulder. When the Day of Resurrection comes, the people will be told, "Enter Paradise", while Uways will be told, "Stop and intercede." God Almighty will then give him the right to intercede for as many people as the tribes of Rabīʿa and Muḍar. ʿUmar, ʿAlī, if you meet him, ask him to pray that God forgive you, and God will forgive you.'

"Ten years passed, and they searched for him to no avail. Then in the year of ‘Umar's death, during the pilgrimage, Sayyidunā ‘Umar went to the mountain of Abū Qubays and yelled at the top of his voice, 'Pilgrims of Yemen, is there anyone among you named Uways?' An old man with a long beard stood up and answered, 'We do not know which Uways you are searching for, but my nephew is named Uways. He is unknown and has no wealth, and is too insignificant to bring him to you. He herds our camels, and is not well respected among us.' ‘Umar said nonchalantly as if he was not much interested, 'Where is that nephew of yours? Is he here in our Sacred Precinct?' He replied 'Yes, he is.' He said, 'Where could I find him?' The man replied, 'On mount ‘Arafāt.'

"So ‘Umar and ‘Alī quickly rode out to ‘Arafāt, where they found Uways praying under a tree with camels grazing around him. They tied their donkeys, approached him and greeted him, 'Peace and the mercy of God be upon you.' Uways cut his prayer short, and replied when he had finished it, 'Peace and the mercy and blessings of God be upon you.'

"They asked him, 'Who are you?' He replied, 'I am a camel herder, working for some people.' They said: 'We are not asking you about your work. What is your name?' He replied, ' I am ‘Abd Allāh (Servant of God).' They said, 'We know that all the people of the heavens and the earth are the servants of God— but what did your mother name you?'

"He said, 'You two! What do you want from me?'

"They replied, 'God's Messenger ﷺ talked once about Uways al-Qaranī. He described his black-blue eyes, and told us that he has a white mark under his left shoulder. Show it to us, so we can know if you are the one we have been seeking.'

"Uways then bared his left shoulder, and they saw a white mark. They rushed to embrace and kiss him, and said: 'We declare that you are Uways al-Qaranī, so ask forgiveness for us, and may God forgive you.'

"He answered: 'I do not devote my prayers for forgiveness to myself, nor to any individual child of Adam; but I ask it for all those on land or sea, the believing men and women, the Muslim men and women. Now, you two—God has told you all about me, but tell me, who are you?"

"'Alī answered, 'This is 'Umar b. al-Khaṭṭāb, the Commander of the Faithful, and I am 'Alī b. Abī Ṭālib.'

"Uways stood up and said, 'Peace, mercy and blessings of God be upon you, Commander of the Faithful, and you 'Alī b. Abī Ṭālib. May God reward you both on behalf of the Muslims.' He replied, 'May God reward you too, on your own behalf.'

"Then 'Umar said, 'Do not leave this place, may God have mercy on you. Allow me to return to Mecca to bring you some of my money and clothing. Let this place be where we meet.'

"Uways answered, "Commander of the Faithful, there will be no further meeting. After this day, I shall not see you again. And tell me: what would I do with money? What would I do with clothes? Don't you see that my shoes are stitched—when do you think I will wear them out? Do you not see that my employers paid me four dirhams—when do you think I will spend them all? Commander of the Faithful, there is a huge obstacle between you and me that can only be traversed by a thin, puny, emaciated man. So be light, may God have mercy on you.'

"When 'Umar heard those words, he threw his purse to the ground and yelled: 'If only 'Umar's mother never gave birth! If only she were barren! Who shall take this, and what it contains?'

"Uways said, 'Commander of the Faithful! Go your way, and I shall go mine.' 'Umar went back to Mecca, and Uways brought back the camels to his people. Then he left his work and devoted himself to worship until he returned to God Almighty."[223]

223 Abū Nu'aym, *Ḥilya* #1606.

4.

The Name (*al-Ism*)

In the Arabic language:

The term *ism* means "a word or expression assigned to someone or something to identify them in speech." [224]

In the Terminology of the Karkariya Order:

It is the manifestation-site of the Named; the original undifferentiation and root of the names; the foundation of the pure meanings, and their secrets. It is that through which the vocable becomes realized without becoming separated from the Named. The Name is neither the Named-in-Itself nor other-than-It, but rather the guide and the Path through the levels of existence to the Essence.

In the Holy Qur'ān:

The word *ism* and its various derivatives are mentioned 71 times in the Qur'ān, including:

---

224 *Al-Muʿjam al-ʿarabī al-asāsī* p. 644.

God says: **So eat of that over which the Name of God has been invoked, if you are believers in His signs.** [225]

God says: **…That they may witness benefits for them and mention the Name of God, during known days, over the four-legged cattle He has provided them.** [226]

God says: **For every community We have appointed a rite, that they might mention the Name of God over the four-legged cattle He has provided them.** [227]

God says: **Were it not for God's repelling people, some by means of others, monasteries, churches, synagogues, and mosques, wherein God's Name is mentioned much, would have been destroyed.** [228]

God says: **[It is] in houses that God has permitted to be raised and wherein His Name is remembered. He is therein glorified, morning and evening.** [229]

God says: **So glorify the Name of thy Lord, the Magnificent!** [230]

God says: **And invoke the Name of thy Lord morning and evening.** [231]

God says: **Glorify the Name of thy Lord, the Most High.** [232]

God says: **Recite in the Name of thy Lord, Who created.** [233]

---

225 Q Anʿām 6:118.
226 Q Ḥajj 22:28.
227 Q Ḥajj 22:34.
228 Q Ḥajj 34:40.
229 Q Nūr 24:36.
230 Q Wāqiʿa 56:96.
231 Q Insān 76:25.
232 Q Aʿlā 87:1.
233 Q ʿAlaq 96:1.

In the Noble Hadith:

It is narrated on the authority of Anas that God's Messenger ﷺ said: "The Last Hour will not come as long as anyone says, *Allāh, Allāh*. [234]

It is also narrated on the authority of Anas that God's Messenger ﷺ said: "The Last Hour will not come until *Allāh, Allāh* is no longer uttered upon the earth." [235]

It is also narrated on the authority of Anas ؓ that God's Messenger ﷺ said: "The Last Hour will not come until *Allāh, Allāh* is no longer uttered upon the earth; and until a woman may pass by some shoes, pick them up and say, 'These belonged to a man;' and until there are fifty women for every one man; and until the rain falls but the earth no longer produces plants." [236]

'Abd Allāh b. Mughaffal narrated that God's Messenger ﷺ said: "*Allāh, Allāh*! By God, I warn you to be careful of my Companions. Do not make them objects of insults after me. Whoever loves them, it is out of love for me that he loves them; and whoever hates them, it is out of hatred for me that he hates them. Whoever offends them, offends me; and whoever offends me, offends God; and whoever offends God, he shall soon be punished." [237]

---

234 Muslim, *Ṣaḥīḥ* #216.
235 Muslim, *Ṣaḥīḥ* #215.
236 Ḥākim, *Mustadrak* #8626.
237 Tirmidhī, *Jāmiʿ* #3827.

✦

The Legal Status of Invoking the Singular Name (*al-Ism al-Mufrad*), Allāh

There is nothing in God's Book, nor in the Sunna of God's Messenger ﷺ, that forbids us from invoking the Singular Name. The contention that the Companions did not invoke this way is not by any means certain, for no one but their Lord knows what they did in their solitary vigils and private supplications, nor the spiritual states that overcame them.

Abū Hurayra said: "I preserved two stores from God's Messenger ﷺ. As for the first one, I have conveyed it; as for the other, if I were to convey it, this throat of mine would be cut." [238] Now it is totally inconceivable to think that Companions refused to transmit certain knowledge, or concealed it, as this hadith seems to suggest. On the contrary, they conveyed knowledge to each individual according to what they could handle, in accordance with the well-known hadith, "Speak to people according to the capacity of their intellects." They conveyed the station of submission (*islām*) to the people of Islam, the station of faith (*īmān*) to the people of faith, and the station of spiritual excellence (*iḥsān*) to the people of spiritual excellence. This ensured that God and His Messenger ﷺ would not be accused of falsehood.

238 Bukhārī, *Ṣaḥīḥ* #118.

So Sayyidunā Abū Hurayra divulged the store of exoteric knowledge to exoteric people, those who are confined to outward meanings. Likewise, he divulged the store of esoteric knowledge to esoteric people, those who delve into the hidden meanings of faith. God says: **Have you not considered that God has made whatsoever is in the heavens and whatsoever is on the earth subservient unto you and has poured His Blessings upon you, both outwardly and inwardly? Among mankind are those who dispute concerning God without knowledge, without guidance, and without an illuminating Book.** [239]

So there are **outward** and **inward blessings**, and the greatest **blessing** God has bestowed upon us is to guide us to His religion.

As for the claim that the revealed Law only recommends invocations that consist of complete meaningful sentences, while the Name of God is an isolated word rather than a full sentence, we can consider the hadith narrated by Abū Hurayra ﷺ in which the Prophet ﷺ said, "God the Exalted says, 'I am as my servant think of Me, and I am with him when he remembers Me. If he remembers Me in himself, I remember him in Myself; if he remembers Me in an assembly, I remember him in a better assembly. If he draws a hand's span nearer Me, I draw an arm's

---

239 Q Luqmān 31:20.

length nearer him; and if he draws an arm's length nearer Me, I draw a fathom nearer him. If he comes to Me walking, I go to him running."[240]

The one who invokes the Singular Name only calls upon God, whether in a group or alone; and God knows what he means, whether he speaks or not. Is it acceptable to think that God requires that invocation and supplication take the form of Arabic words properly conjugated and structured? What about non-Arabic speakers, or mute people, or those uneducated in grammar?

Glory be to our Lord, He Who is not confused by sounds or languages, He Who knows the intentions and desires of every soul with His pre-eternal knowledge! Likewise, mental invocation is not limited by the requirements of linguistics or grammar, but is based on the purity of one's innate disposition (*fiṭra*) and nature (*sajiyya*).

Moreover, the invocation of the Singular Name is a call divested of syntax, as though the invoker were saying, "O Allāh, O Allāh." Consider how God said, **Joseph, turn away from this,**[241] addressing him directly by his name rather than saying *yā Yūsuf*, "O Joseph."

Furthermore, when Umayya b. Khalaf was torturing Sayyidunā Bilāl under the burning sun, Bilāl cried out, *Aḥad, Aḥad*, "One, One!", and the Prophet approved of this and did not censure him.

---

240 Bukhārī, *Ṣaḥīḥ* #6883.
241 Q Yūsuf 12:29.

It is related that someone asked Imam Abū Bakr al-Shiblī (d. 946), "Abū Bakr, why do you say *Allāh* instead of *lā ilāha illā Allāh*?" He answered, "I need not use Him to negate other than Him." The man said, "Tell me more, Abū Bakr." He answered, "My tongue cannot pronounce words of denial." The man repeated, "Tell me more, Abū Bakr." Shiblī answered, "**Say: Allāh, then leave them.**" [242] The man cried out, and fell down dead. His family pursued Shiblī and demanded restitution for him, and took the matter to the Caliph. The Caliph sent a letter to Shiblī demanding that he explain himself. He replied, "A spirit yearned, cried out, was called home, and answered the call. What was my crime?" At this, the Caliph and his retinue cried out and said, "Leave him be, he committed no crime." [243]

In his *Ṣaḥīḥ*, Imam Muslim narrated a hadith on this matter which is authentic and as clear as can be. The hadith tells us that God's Messenger ﷺ said, "The Last Hour will not come as long as anyone says, *Allāh, Allāh*." [244] Why, then, is there any need to interpret this hadith away and change its meaning? How strange it is that someone may spend his life fighting against metaphorical interpretation, but as soon as he encounters a hadith or verse that does not support his school of thought, he suddenly starts twisting meanings around to fit his preconceptions!

---

242 Q Anʿām 6:91.
243 Baqlī, *ʿArāʾis*, vol. 1 p. 383.
244 Muslim, *Ṣaḥīḥ* #216.

✿

Say, Allāh!

God says, **Say, "Allāh," then leave them to play at their vain discourse.** [245]

Sīdī Aḥmad b. ʿAjība commented on this in his *Tafsīr*:

The Sufis cite this verse as a spiritual allusion to solitude, occupying oneself exclusively with God, and paying no regard to the **vanities**, distractions, and turbid things that others worry about. The verse alludes to forsaking these things in order to reach the station of purity; namely witnessing the divine Singularity and clinging to the secrets of the divine Oneness. To this effect, Ibn ʿAṭāʾ Allāh al-Iskandarī describes the people of witnessing as being worthy of witnessing because "they belong to God, and to nothing apart from Him: **Say, "Allāh," then leave them to play at their vain discourse."** Those who do not understand their allusion may criticize them, for they are frozen and halt with the outer meaning. Yet the Qurʾān has not only an outer meaning but an inner meaning which is only understood by those who are lordly (*rabbāniyyūn*), may God benefit us through them, amen. [246]

We say that there is no duality from the perspective of union because in reality there is no existence except that of the Existentiator of existence (*wājid al-wujūd*). For the Real is now as He ever was, and there is nothing with Him. Existents are only

245 Q Anʿām 6:91.
246 Ibn ʿAjība, *al-Baḥr al-madīd* vol. 2 p. 283.

vanishing shadows that do not exist except in the imagination. Thus, there is no existent thing to negate: **All things perish, save His Face.** [247] This means that **all things perish** and pass away **save** the **Face** of the Real, meaning His Essence. All the essences are in reality passing away and vanishing. They have no existence whatsoever, whether now, or in the past, or in the future. They are as dust in the wind.

Abū Hurayra reported that God's Messenger ﷺ said, "The truest word ever uttered by a poet is the verse of Labīd: 'Behold! Everything apart from God is unreal.'" [248]

A poet also said:

Four letters that dazzled my heart,
And dispelled my woes and my worries:

An Alif that acquainted creation with artistry,
A Lām that encouraged self-reproach,

Another Lām adding deep meanings,
And a Hā' inspiring in me love and knowledge.

And we can read in the *Ḥikam*:

How can it be conceived that something veils Him, when He is the One Who manifests everything?

247   Q Qaṣaṣ 28:88.
248   Muslim, *Ṣaḥīḥ* #4194.

How can it be conceived that something veils Him, when He is the one Who is manifest through everything?

How can it be conceived that something veils Him, when He is the One Who is manifest in everything?

How can it be conceived that something veils Him, when He is the One Who is manifest to everything?

How can it be conceived that something veils Him, when He was the Manifest before the existence of anything?

How can it be conceived that something veils Him, when He is more manifest than anything?

How can it be conceived that something veils Him, when He is the One besides Whom there is nothing?

How can it be conceived that something veils Him, when He is nearer to you than anything?

How can it be conceived that something veils Him, when were it not for Him, nothing would exist?

What a strange thing! How could existence manifest in nothingness? Or how could the noneternal exist alongside the Eternal?

*We add to this, "How can it be conceived that something veils
Him, when nothing is comparable to Him?"*

Sīdī Abū Madyan al-Ghawth (may God sanctify his secret) said:

*Say Allāh, and leave existence and all it contains,
If your aspiration is to reach perfection.*

*For in truth, all things besides God
Are nonexistent, whether in sum or in detail.*

*Know that you and all the worlds,
Were it not for Him, would obliterate and dissolve.*

*That which does not exist in and of itself
Cannot possibly exist without Him.*

*The gnostics are annihilated, for they see naught
But the Self-Exalted, the Transcendent,*

*And they see that all else in truth is perishing,
In the present, the past, and the future.*

*So glimpse with your mind, or with your sight:
Do you see anything other than an act of His acts?*

Behold existence from top to bottom,
Through an eye bolstered with reason and discernment;

You will find everything alluding to His Majesty,
Whether it speaks with its voice or its state.

✿

All that is Upon it is Passing Away

Imam Baqlī says in his *Tafsīr*:

God says: **All that is upon it is passing away. And the Face of thy Lord subsists, Possessed of Majesty and Bounty.** [249]

If we ponder the reality of the cosmos and its inhabitants, we perceive the truth of their nonexistence, although on the surface they seem to exist. This is because in reality, something that needs another thing to sustain it is by definition non-existent. The word "existence" is only used for the self-existing being, and how could a contingent being exist through itself, when it has no self to begin with? True existence is eternal existence, which is why God lauds Himself by saying: **And the Face of thy Lord subsists, Possessed of Majesty and Bounty.**

The reality of **subsistence** (*baqā'*) is only assigned to what **subsists** eternally. The existence of that which comes from nothing and returns to nothing is entirely different from He

249 Q Raḥmān 55:26-27.

Who is beginningless and endless. When you witness things as they truly are, you understand that God exists in and of Himself, while creation exists only through Him. Thus you realize the truth of **passing away** and **subsistence**, and the truth of existence and nonexistence.

God gave His creation the capacity to know His beginninglessness and endlessness through witnessing the **passing away** of this lower world and its inhabitants, so that they could attain realization of this knowledge; for subsistence cannot be known unless annihilation is known first.

Imam Junayd was asked about the verse, **All that is upon it is passing away**, and answered: "That which is situated between two edges of annihilation is itself annihilated." [250]

Ibn ʿAṭāʾ Allāh al-Iskandarī (may God sanctify his secret) said:

By His divine grace, God manifested His supreme knowledge and power through His Name, to the extent that the minds of His creatures could bear it, so that they would be linked to Him. By His divine grace, He assigned a particular predisposition to his creation allowing them to know Him, and made them bear witness to what they saw, and they testified to this against themselves when they said, **Yes, indeed**. [251] And now, in the moment of their existence, He calls them to bear witness once more by manifesting to them His Supreme Name, *Allāh*, allowing them to know Him through it, facilitating its remembrance with the tongue, and making it always accessible to them, and manifest-

250 Baqlī, *ʿArāʾis* vol. 3 pp 376-377.
251 Q Aʿrāf 7:172.

ing it clearly to them in **bismi'Llāh al-Raḥmān al-Raḥīm, 'In the Name of God, the All-Merciful, the Ever-Merciful.'** His manifestation is thus so intense that He is hidden, and nothing can describe Him. His remembrance is so abundant that He is forgotten, such that He is no longer recognized. Moreover, it is through Him that affairs are rectified, and it is through His remembrance that difficulty is transformed to ease. Through Him, all needs are fulfilled, and one begins to partake in all secondary causes with Him. He it is Whose heavens and earth could not contain Him, nor His throne, nor His pedestal, but only His will and the hearts of those of His servants for whom He destined good, according to the measure of it which He placed in the hearts of His faithful chosen servants by attributing their servanthood to Him, and unveiling His secret to them. Exalted are His Names![252]

✸

Recite in the Name of the Lord

'Ā'isha ✥ related: "The first revelation given to God's Messenger ✸ was in the form of true dreams in his sleep, which were all as bright and clear as the rising sun. He used to go to the Cave of Ḥirā' and spend many nights there in worship, taking provisions with him, and then return to Khadīja for

---

252 Ibn 'Aṭā', *al-Qaṣd al-mujarrad* pp 33-34. (See Khalid Williams' translation, *Islamic Texts Society*, 2018).

more. This went on until suddenly the truth descended upon him while he was in Ḥirā'. The angel came to him there and told him, 'Recite!' The Prophet ﷺ replied, 'I am not a reciter.'"

[The Prophet ﷺ recalled:] "The angel took hold of me and embraced me until I could not no longer bear it, then released me and said, 'Recite!' I replied, 'I am not a reciter.' He took hold of me a second time and embraced me until I could no longer bear it, then released me and said, 'Recite!' I replied, 'I am not a reciter.' He took hold of me a third time and embraced me until I could no longer bear it, then released me and said, **Recite in the Name of thy Lord Who created, created man from a blood clot. Recite! Thy Lord is most noble, Who taught by the Pen, taught man that which he knew not.**" [253]

['Ā'isha continued:] "Then he returned home with the revelation, trembling with terror. He went in to Khadīja and said, "Cover me! Cover me!" She covered him till his fear was over, and then he said, 'Khadīja, what is wrong with me?' He told her everything that had happened and said, 'I fear for myself.' Khadīja said, 'Never! Rejoice, for by God, God would never disgrace you. You keep good relations with your kin, speak the truth, help the poor and the destitute, serve your guests generously, and assist righteous causes.' Khadīja then accompanied him to her cousin Waraqa, who had become a Christian during the pre-Islamic era and used to write the Gospels in Arabic. He was an old man and had lost his eyesight. Khadīja said to him,

253 Q 'Alaq 96:1-5.

'Cousin! Listen to your nephew's story.' Waraqa asked, 'Nephew, what have you seen?' The Prophet ﷺ described what he had seen. Waraqa said, 'This is the same *Nomos* that was sent down to Moses. I wish I were young and could live to see the day when your people drive you out.' God's Messenger ﷺ asked, 'Will they drive me out?' Waraqa replied, 'Yes. Never did a man bring the like of what you have brought, but that he was treated with hostility. If I should remain alive till your day comes, I will lend you all my support.' But Waraqa died shortly afterwards, and the revelation also paused for a while, until the Prophet ﷺ became so despondent that he almost flung himself from a mountaintop. But whenever he went to the edge to throw himself off, the angel would appear to him and say, 'Muḥammad, you are truly God's Messenger', and this would set his soul at ease, and he would go back. Then after more time passed without any further revelation, he would get into the same state, and it would all happen again." [254]

So the first verse that has ever been revealed was, **Read in the Name of thy Lord.** For the Beloved ﷺ was totally extinguished in the presence of union, immersed in the ocean of divine proximity, and so the presence of the Name knocked upon his blessed heart to remind him of the **reading** of pre-eternity. The *Hamza*, the first letter to be revealed beneath the line, symbolizes the hiddenness of the greatest secret. When his ﷺ heart was opened, the pre-eternal Aḥmadan reality surfaced above the

254 Bukhārī, *Ṣaḥīḥ* #6497.

veils of the line, and so the Muḥammadan image became manifest. This is the secret of why the word *Iqra'*, "**Read**" (إقـرأ), is written with a *Hamza* under the line in the beginning, and another above the line at the end.

So he **read** in the **Name** of His **Lord**, *Allāh*, the Unifying Name that refers to the Essence, the realities of His Existence and the secret of His Essentiality. God says: **Read your book! On this Day, your soul suffices as a reckoner against you.** [255]

Thus, because of God's jealous protectiveness toward His chosen Beloved, he **read** the lines of his pre-eternal being for himself and through himself, so that no one, whether angel, jinn, or man, could ever know the secret existing between him and His Lord.

So the **Name** led him to the Named, and whereas Sayyidunā Adam received the knowledge of the names, Sayyidunā Muḥammad ﷺ received the knowledge of the Named. Because of Him, the gates of eternity were opened, and the deep realities of Oneness and the Lights of Self-Sufficiency poured out.

His **reading** concerned what was beyond knowledge, written upon the page of his essence with the pen of **the Name**. Thus, the way of God's folk who came after him is to invoke the Singular **Name** *Allāh*, in order to ascend through the stages of pre-eternity. Their knowledge lies beyond the stages of worship, and it is for this reason that the majority of people have always

---

255 Q Isrā' 17:14.

rejected and denigrated them, for their minds are limited to a superficial understanding of religious obligations.

To this effect, Sīdī Aḥmad al-ʿAlawī (may God sanctify his secret) said:

O you who wish to know my art,
Ask the Divine about me;

Humans do not recognize me,
For my states are hidden from them.

Seek me in the midst of nearness,
Beyond the state of worship;

As for the world and its containers,
No part of me remains therein.

We also said in a poem of ours:

Invoke the Supreme Name,
And cleave to the spiritual;

Visualize its letters, made of Light,
And fold up your mortal human nature.

The Name and the Named,
Comprise the station of Oneness.

The invocation of the Singular Name is thus one of the foundational principles of the Karkariya Order. It illuminates the disciple's spirit, and gathers together all the divine secrets. He who abandons it leaves the path of the Sufis as well as the Sunna of the Beloved and the Book of God, for there is no **reading** except **in the Name** of God, and **the Name** that brings together all His Attributes and points to His Essence is indeed the Name *Allāh*.

When the disciple masters the visualization of the letters of the **Name**, his heedlessness disappears, relatively if not totally. This visualization is done by means of a wooden tablet that we call *al-wāsiṭa*, which helps the disciple to engrave those letters in his heart. When the luminosity of the **Name's** letters flow through his heart, his human nature will be enfolded spontaneously, because human nature and the letters of the **Name** cannot come together in the same heart. This is the secret of the verse: **Truly God forgives not that any partner be ascribed unto Him, but He forgives what is less than that for whomsoever He will.** [256]

God's jealousy and glory do not allow for the presence of aught besides Him in the station of divinity. If the human nature of the disciple disappears and his heart becomes able to contain all the letters of the Name, he will perceive the secret of the multiplicity of oneness, whereupon that which never existed will pass away, and that which always was will subsist.

---

256 Q Nisā' 4:48.

✿

The Essence (*Dhāt*)

In the Arabic language:

The *dhāt* of something means the thing-in-itself. It is the reality and constituents of an existent, as opposed to the accidents that pertain to it. [257]

In the Terminology of the Karkariya Order:

The Essence is the name for the source of all things, which sustains Itself and cannot be perceived in any respect whatsoever. It cannot be described by existence or nonexistence. It is is the mystery of mysteries, the hidden treasure, and the cause of manifestation of the pluralities of the names, attributes, and qualities, which depend upon it for their nonexistent subsistence.

"Know that the Essence of God is the mystery of Unity, which every symbol expresses in a certain respect, without it being able to express It in many other respects. One does not conceive of It by any rational concept, any more than one understands It by any conventional allusion. For a thing is understood only by means of something that compares to it and thus corresponds to it, or something that negates it and thus opposes it; but there is nothing in existence that compares to the Essence, nor corresponds to It, nor negates It, nor opposes It." [258]

257 *Al-Mu'jam al-'arabī al-asāsī* p. 477.
258 Jīlī, *al-Insān al-kāmil* vol. 1 p. 13.

So understanding and perception are attained through comparison or opposition, but nothing is comparable or opposed to the sublime Essence. From this we can conclude two things. The first is that the inability to perceive is itself perception. A poet said of this:

The inability to perceive is to perceive,
And to search for the secret of the Essence is idolatry.

The hidden depths of human aspirations contain some
That no jinn or angel could hope to perceive.

The second is that the only true existent is God Himself. In this sense, Mūlāy ʿAbd al-Salām b. Mashīsh (d. 1227) ﷺ once said to Mūlāy Abū al-Ḥasan al-Shādhilī ﷺ, "Abū al-Ḥasan, sharpen the eye of faith, and you will find God in everything, at everything, with everything, before everything, after everything, above everything, below everything, near everything, and encompassing everything. You will find Him through a nearness that is His attribute, an encompassment that is His quality, and beyond all containership, limits, spaces and directions. His company and nearness are beyond spatial distances, and His encompassment is beyond encircling His creatures. He erases everything with His very own description: **He is the First, the Last, the Manifest, the Hidden.** He, is He, is He. God was, and there was nothing with Him; and He is now as He ever was."

Imam al-Jīlī said in one of his poems:

The eye cannot see Him, limits cannot confine Him;
Even the one who is near Him cannot describe Him;

The one to whose heart He discloses Himself
Will wear himself out attempting vainly to tell of Him.

Firmament without sphere, spirit without angel,
A King with a kingdom of glory and majesty;

Eye unseeing, knowledge untold,
Deed without effect, traces vanished;

An Essence detached, a singular description,
Verses unfolded, recited by their Author.

Pure existence is His, immaculateness encompasses Him;
He who wakes up from his sleep knows Him, yet knows not.

If you claim to know Him, you give Him not His due;
If you say you know Him not, then you know Him.

My Secret is His ipseity, my spirit His identity,
My heart His throne, my body His servant.

I comprehend Him, yet at once I am ignorant of Him;
The one who attains Him only loses Him.

Two opposites combined in Him and did not repel;
A wellspring flowed, and an ocean gushed forth.

✧

God's Exclusive Unity (*Aḥadiyya*)

In the Terminology of the Karkariya Order:

Aḥadiyya refers to the most exclusive of the unqualified presences of the Essence, and the ultimate erasure of all levels, relations, perspectives, entities and multiplicities. It is hallowed beyond allusion and expression, and wholly self-referential.

Ubayy b. Kaʿb related that the idolaters said to God's Messenger ﷺ, "Muḥammad, what is the lineage of your Lord?" So God revealed: **Say, "He, God, is Exclusively One, God, the Self-Sufficient. He begets not, nor was He begotten. And none is like unto Him."** [259]

All the secrets of *tawḥīd* and the lordly gnostic sciences are enfolded within this surah. As we know, the Qur'ān was revealed with three principal exoteric elements: laws, stories, and doctrine; and Surah *al-Ikhlāṣ* fully encompasses all the foundations

---

259 Q Ikhlāṣ 112:1-4. Aḥmad, *Musnad* #20717.

and levels of *tawḥīd*. Thus, the Prophet 🕋 said: "Is any one of you unable to recite a third of the Qur'an in a night?" The Companions said, "But how could one recite a third of the Qur'ān?" He 🕋 replied, **"Say: He, God, is Exclusively One** is worth a third of the Qur'ān." [260]

According to the science of mystical allusions, the meaning of this is that God was a hidden treasure in pre-eternity, and He loved to be known, and so He created he creation so He could be known. Then He looked into their hearts and saw that they would not be able to know Him because of the obscurity of the link between the contingent and the eternal. So He placed between them and Himself a creature who shared their outward form, and adorned him with compassion and mercy, and forgave him all his past and future deeds, and expanded his heart with Light of *tawḥīd*, and placed lordly eloquence upon his tongue. Through him, the Lord opened the gates of eternity. He unveiled to Him the source of reality itself, and commanded him to acquaint His creatures with Him.

Thus, He said to him, **Say** (*qul*), O Muḥammad. The *Qāf* was the first letter sent down, overwhelming (*qāhira*) the non-eternity of creation through the secret of the Real's eternity, and manifesting the magnificence of eternity over non-eternity.

Then He said, **He** (*huwa*), and the hearts of people of *tawḥīd* became lost in the valleys of bewilderment and confusion when the magnificence of the divine Identity (*huwiyya*)

---

260 Muslim, *Ṣaḥīḥ* #1350.

appeared to them, and the pillars upon which they based their existence shook and collapsed. He annihilated them forever, so that the inmost core of divinity remained hallowed beyond any association.

Thereupon, He manifested His all-encompassing Name **Allāh, God**, which denotes the Essence. They discerned the *Lām* of Magnificence (*lām al-ʿaẓama*) and fell down in prostration, and then the *Lām* of Love (*lām al-ʿishq*), and they melted with yearning and desire. Then He unveiled the singularity of the *Alif*, and they acknowledged their incapacity to perceive Him. Everything that was in motion within them fell still, and they became erased in the essence of union.

Thereupon, the omnipotent power of *al-Aḥad*, **the Exclusively One,** disclosed itself, and all perspectival multiplicity and particular relativity crumbled to dust; and there was no more to tell of them, nor anyone to tell it.

Sīdī Ibn ʿAjība says in his *Tafsīr*:

The shaykh of our shaykhs Sīdī ʿAbd al-Raḥmān al-ʿĀrif said: "In sum, the allusion of **He** (*huwa*) is specific to those who have drowned and attained true realization of He-ness (*huwiyya*). When the ocean of **exclusive oneness** (*aḥadiyya*) engulfed them, and true existence was unveiled to them, they found no one to make reference to but Him. For that to which reference is made is One, and the allusion must therefore be nondelimited and can only refer to Him. After all, they lost awareness of anything but Him, passed away from all human traces, and became absent from their own existence, senses, and engendered qualities. This is the true meaning of *tawḥīd* and exaltation. May God grant us this at all times, and make us worthy of it, through the blessing of His Prophet ﷺ. All success is from God, and may God bless our master Muḥammad and his family."[261]

Imam Qushayrī says in his *Tafsīr*:

It has been said that the Surah explains itself: Who is **He**? **He is God.** Who is **God**? **God** is the **Exclusively One.** Who is the **Exclusively One**? He is the **Self-Sufficient.** Who is the **Self-Sufficient**? He is **the One Who neither begets nor was begotten.** Who is **the One Who neither begets nor was begotten**? He is **the One Who has no like unto Him.**

It has also been said that He revealed to the innermost secrets by saying, **He,** and to the spirits by saying, **God,** and to the hearts by saying, **Exclusively One,** and to the souls of the believers with the rest of the surah.

Others said that He revealed to the lovers by saying, **He,** and to the monotheists by saying, **God,** and to the gnostics by saying, **Exclusively One,** and to the scholars by saying, **the Self-Sufficient,** and to the intellectuals by saying, **He begets not, nor was He begotten,** and so on.[262]

Sīdī ʿAbd al-Salam b. Mashīsh (may God sanctify his secret) said in his famous prayer upon the Prophet, "Plunge me into the oceans of **exclusive unity** (*biḥār al-aḥadiyya*)." By this, he meant the ocean of the Essence, which is hallowed beyond the

---

261 Ibn ʿAjība, *al-Baḥr al-madīd* vol. 8 p. 373.
262 Qushayrī, *Laṭāʾif al-ishārāt* vol. 3 p. 783.

waves of the Names and Attributes, where there are no longer any perspectives, determinations, relations, allusions, effects, or traces.

In the science of the Sufis, there is distinction between "exclusive oneness" (*Aḥadiyya*) and "inclusive oneness" (*Wāḥidiyya*), because *Aḥadiyya* comes from *Aḥad* ("one" in the sense of "one and only") while *Wāḥidiyya* comes from *Wāḥid* ("one" in the sense of "the one"). *Aḥadiyya* is above *Wāḥidiyya* because it refers to the Essence alone, erasing all the connections of the Names and Attributes. *Wāḥidiyya*, for its part, refers to the Essence along with the Names and Attributes inside the circle of the Essence's identity, in the sense that each one is the other.

Imam al-Jīlī said: "*Aḥadiyya* is the disclosure-site of 'God was, and there was nothing with Him', and *Wāḥidiyya* is the disclosure-site of 'and He is now as He ever was.'" [263]

All we have said of *Aḥadiyya* here is merely an approximation, not a definition, because from the perspective of the verified truth, nothing can be said about it.

---

263 Jīlī, *al-Insān al-kāmil* p. 49.

✦

The *Hāʾ* of Identity (*Hāʾ al-huwiyya*)

In the Terminology of the Karkariya Order:

Huwiyya is the uncreated reality that manifests through non-delimited existence, and the universal encompassment of being.

If we erase the *Alif* (ا) and the two *Lāms* (ل) of the Name *Allāh* (الله), only the letter *Hāʾ* (ﻪ) remains, along with an unwritten *Wāw*, making *huwa*, "He," an allusion to the Oneness of the Real.

God says: **But He is God, my Lord, and I ascribe none as partner unto my Lord.** [264]

God says: **Had God wanted to take a child, He would have chosen whatsoever He willed from that which He created. Glory be to Him; He is the One, the Paramount.** [265]

God says: **He is God, other than Whom there is no god, Knower of the Unseen and the seen. And He is the Compassionate, the Merciful. He is God, other than Whom there is no god, the Sovereign, the Holy, Peace, the Faithful, the Protector, the Mighty, the Compeller, the Proud. Glory be to Him above the partners they ascribe. He is God, the Creator, the Maker, the Fashioner; unto Him belong the Most Beautiful Names. Whatsoever is in the heavens and the earth glorifies Him, and He is the Mighty, the Wise.** [266]

264 Q Kahf 18:38.
265 Q Zumar 39:4.
266 Q Ḥashr 59: 22-24.

God says: **Say, "He, God, is Exclusively One."** [267]

The word *huwa* alludes to the divine primacy and ultimacy. The letter *Hā'* comes from the deepest place of the throat, while the *wāw* is pronounced with the lips. When saying *huwa*, the mouth is always open, symbolizing pre-eternity. *Huwa* is the first divine Name listed in the hadith of the ninety-nine Names:

Abū Hurayra narrated that God's Messenger ﷺ said, "Verily God has ninety-nine names, one hundred minus one; for He is Odd, and He loves the odd. Whosoever reckons them will enter Paradise. He (*huwa*) is God, there is no god but He, the All-Merciful (*al-Raḥmān*), the Ever-Merciful (*al-Raḥīm*), the King (*al-Malik*), the Holy (*al-Quddūs*), the Peace (*al-Salām*), the Faithful (*al-Mu'min*), the Overseer (*al-Muhaymin*), the Mighty (*al-ʿAzīz*), the All-Compelling (*al-Jabbār*), the Self-Great (*al-Mutakabbir*), The Creator (*al-Khāliq*), the Maker (*al-Bāri'*), the Form-Giver (*al-Muṣawwir*), the All-Forgiving (*al-Ghaffār*), the Subjugator (*al-Qahhār*), the Bestower (*al-Wahhāb*), the Provider (*al-Razzāq*), the All-Opening (*al-Fattāḥ*), the Knowing (*al-ʿAlīm*), the Contractor (*al-Qābiḍ*), the Expander (*al-Bāsiṭ*), the Lowerer (*al-Khāfiḍ*), the Uplifter (*al-Rāfiʿ*), the Exalter (*al-Muʿizz*), the Abaser (*al-Mudhill*), the Hearing (*al-Samīʿ*), the Seeing (*al-Baṣīr*), the Ruler (*al-Ḥakam*), the Just (*al-ʿAdl*), the Gentle (*al-Laṭīf*), the Aware (*al-Khabīr*), the Forbearing (*al-Ḥalīm*), the Tremendous (*al-ʿAẓīm*), the Forgiving (*al-Ghafūr*), the Grateful (*al-Shakūr*), the High (*al-ʿAlī*), the Great (*al-Kabīr*), the Guardian (*al-Ḥafīẓ*), the Nour-

---

267 Q Ikhlāṣ 112:1.

isher (*al-Muqīt*), the Reckoner (*al-Ḥasīb*), the Majestic (*al-Jalīl*), the Generous (*al-Karīm*), the Watchful (*al-Raqīb*), the All-Embracing (*al-Wāsiʿ*), the Wise (*al-Ḥakīm*), the Loving (*al-Wadūd*), the Glorious (*al-Majīd*), the Responder (*al-Mujīb*), the Upraiser (*al-Bāʿith*), the Witness (*al-Shahīd*), the Real (*al-Ḥaqq*), the Trustee (*al-Wakīl*), the Strong (*al-Qawī*), the Firm (*al-Matīn*), the Friend (*al-Walī*), the Praised (*al-Ḥamīd*), the Enumerator (*al-Muḥṣī*), the Originator (*al-Mubdiʾ*), the Returner (*al-Muʿīd*), the Life-Giver (*al-Muḥyī*), the Death-Causer (*al-Mumīt*), the Living (*al-Ḥayy*), the Self-Subsisting (*al-Qayyūm*), the Finder (*al-Wājid*), the Glorified (*al-Mājid*), the One (*al-Wāḥid*), the Only (*al-Aḥad*), the Self-Sufficient (*al-Ṣamad*), the Powerful (*al-Qādir*), the Potent (*al-Muqtadir*), He Who Brings Forward (*al-Muqaddim*), He Who Delays (*al-Muʾakkhir*), the First (*al-Awwal*), the Last (*al-Ākhir*), the Manifest (*al-Ẓāhir*), the Nonmanifest (*al-Bāṭin*), the Transcendent (*al-Mutaʿāl*), the Source of Goodness (*al-Barr*), the Acceptor of Repentance (*al-Tawwāb*), the Avenger (*al-Muntaqim*), the Pardoner (*al-ʿAfū*), the Kind (*al-Raʾūf*), Owner of the Kingdom (*Mālik al-Mulk*), Possessor of Majesty and Bounty (*Dhul-Jalāl wal-Ikrām*), the Equitable (*al-Muqsiṭ*), the Gatherer (*al-Jāmiʿ*), the Independent (*al-Ghanī*), the Enricher (*al-Mughnī*), the Preventer (*al-Māniʿ*), the Cause of Harm (*al-Ḍarr*), the Cause of Benefit (*al-Nāfiʿ*), the Light (*al-Nūr*), the Guide (*al-Hādī*), the Sublime Maker (*al-Badīʿ*), the Everlasting (*al-Bāqī*), the Inheritor (*al-Wārith*), the Right-Guider (*al-Rashīd*), the Patient (*al-Ṣabūr*)."[268]

---

268 Ibn Ḥibbān, *Ṣaḥīḥ* #815.

It has been said that the following verse contains the sum of all knowledge: **He is God, other than Whom there is no god** (*huwa Allāh alladhī lā ilāha illā huwa*).[269] These words begin and end with the word *huwa*, symbolizing how all knowledge is contained in the *huwiyya*.

It is narrated that Imam Junayd (may God sanctify his secret) once said to one of his closest followers: "The Supreme Name of God, is *huwa*, because God first manifested it in his Name *Allāh*, and hid it at the end of the *Hā'* of this Name. It is *huwa*, and it was so clearly manifest that it became hidden and no longer recognized, and so oft-repeated that it was forgotten and no longer remarked upon."[270]

Ibn ʿAṭā' Allāh al-Iskandarī explains in his work *Pure Intention: On Knowledge of the Unique Name* (*al-Qaṣd al-mujarrad fī maʿrifat al-ism al-mufrad*) that the Verse of the Throne (*Āyat al-Kursī*) is the foremost verse of the Qur'ān because the letter *Hā'* appears in it eleven times, each time in reference to the divine Essence, and it also contains the Name of the Essence both explicitly and implicitly in its *Hā'* pronouns. Ibn ʿAṭā' also says in this book:

It is related that Abū Bakr al-Shiblī (may God have mercy on him) said, "I came across a lively young Ethiopian girl who was running and racing about. I said to her, 'Maidservant of God, calm down and be easy on yourself.' She replied, *'Huwa, huwa.'* I said to her, 'Where did you come from?' She replied, *'Huwa.'*

269 Q Ḥashr 59: 22.
270 Ibn ʿAtā' Illāh, *al-Qaṣd al-mujarrad* p. 56.

I said, 'Where are you going?' She replied, '*Huwa.*' I said, 'What do you want from *Huwa*?' She replied, '*Huwa.*' I said, 'What is your name?' She replied, '*Huwa.*' I said, 'How many times have you said *Huwa* now?' She replied, 'I will keep on saying *Huwa* until I meet *Huwa.*' Then she said,

Ah my beloved, I have no replacement for you,
And I have nothing else to seek but you.

Because of my madness for you, they called me sick,
And I answered: I hope I am never cured!'"

Al-Shiblī continued: "So I said to her, 'Maidservant of God, what do you mean by *Huwa*? Do you mean God?' But when she heard the Name of God, she took an enormous gasp and fell down dead – may God have mercy on her! I wanted to take her away to be prepared for burial, but a voice called out, 'Shiblī! If someone goes mad out of love for Us, and seeks Us with ardour and invokes Us with passion, and dies by Our Name, then leave them for Us, for We shall pay their bounty.' I looked to see who was calling, and she had disappeared when I looked back. I do not know if she was raised up or buried. May God have mercy on her." [271]

271 Ibid, p. 62.

Ibn 'Aṭā' also says:

It is said that the *tawḥīd*-voicers are divided into four categories. The first group are those who say, *Lā ilāha illā Allāh*, which is a balance of negation and affirmation: a negation of doubts and misunderstandings, and an affirmation of the One beyond any partners or opposites.

The second group are those who say, *Allāh*, invoking only the Singular Name without any negation; they deem that affirming after negating is alienation and estrangement.

The third group are those who say, *Huwa, Huwa*, which is pure affirmation, a constant invocation that is Light on the tongue; it is the invocation of the heart.

The fourth group are those who are silent and say nothing at all, absorbed in Him and oblivious to their own selves, lost in their witnessing of the One Invoked. Their invocation of *tawḥīd* is an act of eye-witnessing, not a deed of the tongue.[272]

✦

The *Lām* of Love or Contraction
(*Lām al-'ishq, Lām al-qabḍ*)

In the Terminology of the Karkariya Order:

The Lām of passion is the secret of the contraction that unifies all directions and annihilates all vestiges. It is the manifes-

---

272 Ibid, p. 58.

tation-site of the uncreated realities, and the center of pure universal meanings.

Removing the *Alif* and the first *Lām* from *Allāh*, we are left with *lahū* (لـه), "to Him, for Him, His", representing love.

God says: **Dost thou not know that unto God (lahū) belongs Sovereignty over the heavens and the earth, and that you have neither protector nor helper apart from God?** [273]

God says: **Dost thou not know that unto God (lahū) belongs sovereignty over the heavens and the earth? He punishes whomsoever He will, and He forgives whomsoever He will. And God is Powerful over all things.** [274]

God says: **Truly unto God (lahū) belongs Sovereignty over the heavens and the earth. He gives life and causes death. Apart from God you have neither protector nor helper.** [275]

God says: **Say, "Unto God belongs intercession altogether. To Him (lahū) belongs sovereignty over the heavens and the earth. Then unto Him shall you be returned."** [276]

God says: **Blessed is He unto Whom (lahū) belongs sovereignty over the heavens and the earth and whatsoever is between them, and with Whom lies knowledge of the Hour, and unto Whom you will be returned.** [277]

---

273 Q Baqara 2:107.
274 Q Mā'ida 5:40.
275 Q Tawba 9:116.
276 Q Zumar 39:44.
277 Q Zukhruf 43:85.

God says: **Unto Him (*lahū*) belongs sovereignty over the heavens and the earth. He gives life and causes death, and He is Powerful over all things.** [278]

God says: **Unto Him (lahū) belongs sovereignty over the heavens and the earth; and God is Witness over all things.** [279]

Because of the majesty of the *Lām* of Dominion (*Lām al-mulk*), the letter is doubled (*mushaddada*) and extended (*mamdūda*), manifesting the flow of the *Alif* and alerting the disciple to the Qibla of pre-eternity.

The *Lām* of Dominion is indeed the manifestation-site of the Perfect Man (*al-insān al-kāmil*), who is the innermost secret of all entities and the gatherer of cosmic realities, created **in the best stature.** [280] He is the first number, a transcription of the Archetypal Book, the manifestation of the shadow of the Supreme Name, the container of the levels of existence. He is the core of the shining path, the supreme presence of union. To this effect, a poem once said:

The secret of the Alif flows in the Lām just the same,
So seek it out, and look beyond the forms.

The secrets of mystical knowledge are gathered in the Lāms,
Like the sun rising at the break of dawn.

---

278 Q Ḥadīd 57:2.
279 Q Burūj 85:7.
280 Q Tīn 95:4.

The Lām tells that creation sits on the edge
Of the Alif, beyond any doubt or denial.

Seek the wisdom that lies within the Lām,
And understand its meanings, if you are among those who reflect.

You will find a reality that once was veiled,
A magnificent treasure, hidden from humankind. [281]

✪

The *Lām* of Gnosis (*Lām al-maʿrifa*)

In the Terminology of the Karkariya Order:
It is the state of dissolving in the water of transcendent love, manifested by the expansion of the mind', so that it may bear the burden of the descent of divine secrets.

If the *Alif* is removed from the divine Name, we are left with *li'Llāh* (الله), "to God, for God, God's."

God says: **Nay, whosoever submits his face to God (*li'Llāh*), while being virtuous, shall have his reward with his Lord. No fear shall come upon them; nor shall they grieve.** [282]

God says: **The fools among the people will say, "What has turned them away from the *qibla* they had been following?"**

---

281 Ibn ʿAṭāʾ Allāh, *al-Qaṣd al-Mujarrad* p. 53.
282 Q Baqara 2:112.

Say, "To God (*li'Llāh*) belong the East and the West. He guides whomsoever He will unto a straight path."[283]

God says: So if they dispute with thee, say, "I submit my face to God (*li'Llāh*), and so too those who follow me."[284]

God says: [...Those] who responded to God (*li'Llāh*) and the Messenger after being afflicted by wounds; for those among them who have been virtuous and reverent there shall be a great reward.[285]

God says: Say, "Unto whom belongs whatsoever is in the heavens and on the earth?" Say: Unto God (*li'Llāh*).[286]

God says: On that Day the earth shall be changed into other than the earth, and the heavens [too], and they will appear before God (*li'Llāh*), the One, the Paramount.[287]

God says: Have they not considered that whatsoever God has created casts its shadow to the right and to the left, prostrating to God (*li'Llāh*) while in a state of abject humility?[288]

This *Lām* is the *Lām* of expansion (*basṭ*), the presence of love and passion, the presence of total fervor for the Beloved and the complete shedding of personal identity, so that the secret of dominion flows and the humanity of the seeker is pulled back to reveal the divinity of the Sought, and its commanding reality (*ḥaqīqat al-amriyya*) is made plain through imminence and

283 Q Baqara 2:142.
284 Q Āl 'Imrān 3:20.
285 Q Āl 'Imrān 3:172.
286 Q An'ām 6:12.
287 Q Ibrāhīm 14:48.
288 Q Naḥl 16:48.

transcendence. Thus Qays, the lover of renown, is said to have wandered bewildered in the desert crying, "I am Layla!"

One of the most beautiful verses on love was composed by Sīdī Ibn al-Fāriḍ, may God sanctify his secret:

Increase me ever in bedazzled love for You,
And have mercy on the body that burns with Your adoration,

And if I should ask to gaze upon You for real,
Permit me, and tell me not, "You shall not see." [289]

Dear heart! You promised me you would be patient
For their love, so beware lest you shrink and contract!

Truly love is life, so die of love;
For it is your right to die, and be excused.

He also said:

It is love, so save yourself, for passion is not easy;
No rational man would choose to be consumed by it.

---

289 A Qur'ānic reference to God's answer to Moses when he asked to see God (Q Aʿrāf 7:143).

Live without it, for even love's repose is toil;
Its beginning is sickness, and its end is death.

And Sīdī Muḥammad al-Ḥarrāq (d. 1845, may God sanctify his secret) said:

Ask love about me: am I a mere pretender?
For love knows well the state of my passion.

It certainly knows that I have loved ones
Whom I love truly, not with affectation.

By God, in truth I am their slave;
I am not a poor man by any means,

For I am rich and mighty through them,
And they have made me renowned in every gathering.

It is pride enough for me to have them as masters,
And to know that I may see and hear them.

✧

The Cloud (*al-ʿamāʾ*)

In the Terminology of the Karkariya Order:

The cloud is the bewilderment of bewilderment, where there is nothing and yet all things.

Abū Razīn al-ʿAqīlī once asked the Prophet ﷺ, "Messenger of God, will we see our Lord on the Day of Resurrection?" He replied, "Do you see the moon when it is full? Or do you see the sun when there are no clouds?" They said, "Yes, Messenger of God." He said, "Then God is mightier still." Abū Razīn said, "Messenger of God, where was our Lord before He created the heavens and the earth?" He replied, "He was in a Cloud, with no air above it, and no air below it."[290]

It is a presence of negation, a presence so bewildering that bewilderment itself is bewildered in bewilderment. It is a presence of "no" (*mā*), as the noble hadith says, "no air above it, and no air below it." The written form of the word *ʿamāʾ* (عماء) both begins and ends with the letter *Hamza*, in the sense that the letter *ʿAyn* (ع) resembles a *Hamza* (ء) when it is joined to the letter that follows it. Then there is the *Mīm* of negation, *mā* (ما), extending into the isthmus between them.

Now the word *ʿamāʾ* may be read in two ways, one separated and the other joined.

290 Ibn Ḥibbān, *Ṣaḥīḥ* #6275.

The separated reading is the presence of *'ayn mā'* (عٰما). The numeric value of the letter *'Ayn* is 70, which is the number of veils between God and creation. In this reading, it is read aloud as *'ayn mā'*, representing the source and wellspring of life, and the eye that sheds a drop of water that separates from and leaves its source, becoming the flow and the meaning of the separated reading, so that the *'ayn* remains free of all that separates from it. [291]

The joined reading is the presence of *'amā'* (عـماء), which in Arabic means a cloud that is dispersed and fine, not limited to any specific place. This cloud bears water, wherein lies the life of all things. If you examine a cloud close up, you find that it is barely a tangible thing at all, like dust in the wind; yet it carries within it the secret of all life.

Observe, then, the beautiful expression of the Master of Creation ﷺ and how with a single word, he combined all these tremendous levels and subtle secrets of divinity.

For this reason, the Cloud is the isthmus of bewilderment, like an imaginary line between a thing and its shadow, neither existent nor nonexistent, neither known nor unknown, neither itself nor something else. It separates and unites opposites; it is the disclosure-site of separation and union.

Anas b. Mālik narrated that God's Messenger ﷺ performed the midday prayer, then sat down in the place where Jibrīl usu-

---

291 In addition to being the name of the letter, *'ayn* is also a word meaning "spring", "source", or "eye", and the word *mā'* means "water", hence this abundance of meanings.

ally visited him. Then Bilāl came and called the *azan* for the afternoon prayer, and the Prophet ﷺ said, 'Those of you who have family in Medina, go take care of your business and perform ablutions.' A few people remained in the mosque; Emigrants from Mecca who had no family in Medina. God's Messenger ﷺ went to them carrying a jug with a little water in the bottom. He tried to put his hand in the container, but it was too narrow, so he put in four fingers. Then he said, 'Come forth and perform ablutions.' So they did, one by one, until they had all finished." When asked how many men there were, Anas replied, "Between seventy and eighty." [292]

This blessed hadith shows us a great spiritual allusion. From his noble fingers—four of them, to be precise—the miraculous water gushed forth. Note that the number of men who performed ablutions was the same as the number of veils separating God from creation. Thus, the Prophet ﷺ alluded to the secret of his own Qur'ānic essence, and the secret of the discriminating nature (*furqāniyya*) of his Companions.

---

292 Aḥmad, *Musnad* #12184.

✿

The *Alif* of *Tawḥīd*

In the Terminology of the Karkariya Order:
It is the vicegerent on the earth of the eternal Muḥammadan existence, the path of primordial Aḥmadan uprightness,
the manifestation-site of divine Oneness, and the secret
of Singularity.

The Alif has virtue and ascendance over
The other letters, so seek no substitute.

The most secret of knowledge is found within it;
Truly unique in its majesty, and unbending;

Eternally upright, one in number,
Its form encompasses the sum and the parts.

Letter and meaning brought together in secret;
Root and branch connected and joined.

Discover its secrets, if you have ambition;
Take its subtleties to heart, and ascend.

It is like a man whose nature embodies
Sublime knowledge, spirit, body and character,

An angel's intellect, an animal's instinct;
How glorious to know it, how dreadful to know not![293]

The *Alif* is the essence and source of the other letters, and the secret of their manifestation in the earth of letters. Thus it is God's vicegerent in the earth of letters, and has the position therein that the number one has among the numbers, with its course and its levels. It is with the *Alif* that God invokes Himself, for it is the manifestation-site of the transcendent Breath, and the locus of "God was, and there was nothing with Him." He is transcendent beyond connecting to another letter, or being described in terms of letters.

Ibn ʿArabī said, may God sanctify his secret:

O Alif of the Essence, transcendent be you,
Have you any source or locus in the cosmos?

It replied, "None, save for my regard;
I am an everlasting letter wherein eternity is contained;

I am but a weak chosen servant,
Yet my authority is mighty and vast."

---

293 Ibn ʿAṭāʾ Allāh, *al-Qaṣd al-mujarrad* pp 50-51.

✿

The Treasure-Dot (*nuqṭat al-kanziyya*)

In the Terminology of the Karkariya Order:

It is the uncompounded root of the root, the Treasure's underlying substrate, and the pre-eternal ink of unitive witnessing.

It is the most distinguished manifestation of essential divine Oneness. For all secondary branches are precluded by its subsistence, and the accident comes to naught through its existence, such that the part is identical to the whole.

It is thus the supreme element, hallowed beyond all form. It is receptive of manifestation in all possible and impossible forms, for it is the secret of the letter, and the inner reality of the line.

The Dot is the quiddity of the very source itself; the origin and substance of matter in which all the sources of the universe gush forth. The Dot is the axis of all circles, because it is the essence of union and the secret of secrets. It is the very reality of the Beloved ﷺ, for it is the Aḥmadan Essence, hallowed beyond expression, description, or speech. Letters are unable to take on its shape out of bashfulness before the beauty of his presence, and oceans of ink have been exhausted in homage to the majesty of his splendor.

5.

Wandering (*siyāḥa*)

In the Arabic language:

The word *siyāḥa* means travelling the land, whether for worship, enjoyment, or observation.

In the Terminology of the Karkariya Order:

Siyāḥa is a non-spatial journey in space, and a timeless journey in time. [294] It is done on the principle of disengagement from other-than-God (*tajrīd*) and ascension through the levels of divine self-sufficiency (*ṣamadiyya*), all the while contemplating the signs of divine power. Its purpose is to achieve the negation of other-than-God and everything that hinders the disciple from Him, and to break through the subtle veils and attain a taste of divine attraction (*jadhba*). This is based on the circular vibrations of passionate love, inside the realm of possibility, so that the idol of the ego may be broken.

---

294 Translator's note: Literally, "to roam in space without a location, and to fare in time without a duration."

In the Holy Qur'ān:

The word *siyāḥa* is mentioned three times in the Holy Qur'ān in different morphological forms, including God's words:

God says: **The penitent, and the worshippers, and the celebrants of praise, and the wanderers (sā'iḥūn), and those who bow, and those who prostrate, and those who enjoin right, and those who forbid wrong, and those who maintain the limits set by God; and give glad tidings unto the believers.** [295]

God says: **So wander freely (sīḥū) throughout the land for four months, and know that you cannot thwart God, and that God shall disgrace the disbelievers.** [296]

In the Noble Hadith:

Abū Umāma ﷺ narrated that a certain man said, "Messenger of God, permit me to go wandering." He answered, "The wandering of my community is jihad in God's cause." [297]

Ibn Mas'ūd related that God's Messenger ﷺ said, "God has angels who wander across the land conveying greetings of peace from my community." [298]

Abū Hurayra reported that God's Messenger ﷺ said, "God has angels who wander about the earth in addition to the ones who record the deeds of mankind. When they find people invoking God, they call out to one another, 'Hasten to what you

---

295 Q Tawba 9:112.
296 Q Tawba 9:2.
297 Ḥākim, *Mustadrak* #2333.
298 Ibn Ḥibbān, *Ṣaḥīḥ* #922.

seek!' Then they come and spread their wings over them up to the first heaven. God Almighty says, 'What were My servants doing when you left them?' They reply, 'When we left them they were praising You, exalting You, and glorifying You.' He says, 'And have they ever seen Me?' They reply, 'No.' He says, 'How would it be if they had seen Me?' They reply, 'Had they seen You, they would glorify You, exalt You, and praise You even more fervently.' God then says, 'For what do they ask?' They reply, 'Paradise.' He says, 'And have they ever seen it?' They reply, 'No.' He says, 'How would it be if they had seen it?' They reply, 'Had they seen it, they would desire it even more.' He says to them, 'From what do they seek refuge?' They reply, 'From Hell.' He says, 'And have they ever seen it?' They reply, 'No.' He says, 'How would it be if they had seen it?' They reply, 'Had they seen it, they would be even more eager to flee from it and avoid it.' Then He says, 'I call you to witness that I have forgiven them.' They say, 'There was a man among them who was not one of them, but had only come to them for some need of his.' God says, 'No one who keeps the company of such people will be disappointed.'" [299]

299 Tirmidhī, *Jāmi'* #3554.

✪

Wandering with the Body and with the Spirit

Dear disciple, you should know that since all of existence is one within the circles of possibility, the locus of spatial confinement (*taḥayyuz*) is also one within the human world (*ʿālam al-nāsūt*), or what is called the world of corporeal bodies (*al-ashbāḥ al-jismāniyya*) or the physical world (*al-mulk*), which is the world of the six sensory directions.

He who is imprisoned by his sensory perceptions and limited to his own body, is part of the physical world. As for he whose heart is opened to the world of Lights, and whose eye (*ʿayn*) is not clouded by the obscuring dot of *ghayn* (غ), so that the moon of gnosis and the suns of subtleties are visible to him, and he sees the cosmos as pure Light—such a person is in the spiritual world.

Now all of these worlds share the same locus, and there is no sequential ordering or spatial elevation. On the contrary, their hierarchal degrees is suprasensory, because the locus is one, but it is seen from differing viewpoints. For example, consider three people trading in a market. The first one only sees people, fruits and vegetables; the second sees God's Light wherever he turns; and the third is totally extinguished in the Lights. Anyone who looks at these men will see them in the same place at the same time, yet there is a world of difference between them.

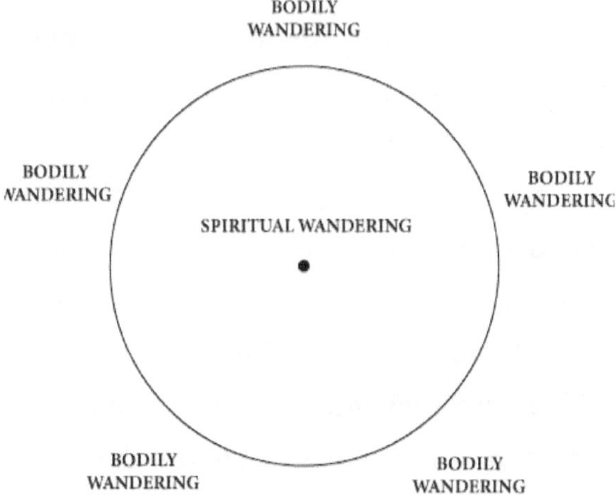

The *siyāḥa* of the body is the journey around the circumference of the circle of all-possibility, accompanied by meditation upon the beauty of creation in order to touch the Qāf of the heart (*qalb*), so that the disciple can penetrate it and access its core.

The purpose of this physical *siyāḥa* is to behold the signs of God's mighty power, as well as to prevent the heart from leaning on the pillars and pleasures of the lower self, as mentioned in the following verse: **Say, "If your fathers, your children, your brothers, your spouses, your tribe, the wealth you have acquired, commerce whose stagnation you fear, and dwellings you find pleasing are more beloved to you than God, and His Messenger, and striving in His way, then wait till God comes with His Command." And God guides not iniquitous people.** [300]

300 Q Tawba 9:24.

Let us focus on His words, **and dwellings you find pleasing.** The word *masākin* (**dwellings**) is from *sukūn*, "stillness." Now for common people, stillness is poor conduct because they are bereft of the Light of witnessing, which is the celestial mount of spiritual wandering. This is why movement is obligatory for them in order to draw nearer to their Lord, in the spirit of the Holy Saying, "Whoever comes to Me walking, I will go to him running." Therefore, they must walk and wander through the physical world in order to turn the wheel that will draw the water of passionate love into the innermost depths of their hearts.

Ibn ʿAjība says in *al-Bahr al-madīd*:

Emigration (*hijra*) from the lands of heedlessness is obligatory, as is separating from those kinsfolk and friends who do not help the servant on his Path to God. The disciple must emigrate from the land where he does not find his heart, and where there is no one to help him with his relation with his Lord, no matter where it may be. I have never seen someone become a saint after remaining in his own homeland, with very few exceptions.

The Prophet ﷺ emigrated from his homeland to Medina, and it was then that the religion was granted success. This has remained the way of the saints ever since, and it is rare to find a saint who succeeds without leaving his home. The disciple must also avoid those who distract him, whether they be parents, children, spouses, or relatives. The same applies to all matters of property and business that distract the heart from God.

This applies, of course, only after he fulfills the rights of his children as mandated by the Sacred Law.

The intelligent disciple is the one who finds the middle way between the revealed Law (*sharīʿa*) and the esoteric Reality (*ḥaqīqa*), without neglecting those who depend on him, whether his spouse or otherwise. He should invoke God all the while, and remain with them in body but depart from them in heart. If he is unable to do so but still wishes to find the remedy for his heart, then he should leave the decision up to his wife, and appoint someone to take care of his family while he strengthens his heart and advances with his Lord. [301]

As for he who has no part in the spiritual *siyāḥa*, he should redouble his efforts in the bodily *siyāḥa* until he masters the different degrees of wayfaring such as hunger, patience, asceticism, turning the other cheek, bearing abuse, and reliance on God. Without this, *siyāḥa* is nothing more than a movement from one created realm to another. It is written in the *Ḥikam*, "Travel not from creature to creature, for otherwise you will be like a donkey at the mill: roundabout he turns, always ending up back where he started. Rather, travel from creation to the Creator. **The ultimate end is unto thy Lord.** [302] Consider the Prophet's ﷺ words, 'Whosoever emigrates for God and His Prophet, his emigration is indeed for God and His Prophet. And whosoever emigrates for worldly benefit, or for a woman he would marry, his emigration is for no more than that.' Under-

---

301 See Ibn ʿAjība's commentary on Q Tawba 9:23-24 in *al-Baḥr al-madīd*.
302 Q Najm 53:42.

stand his ﷺ words, and contemplate this, if you are a person of understanding."

Ibn ʿAjība says in his commentary on the *Ḥikam*: [303]

He who travels from one created realm to another is the one who travels from other-than-God in search of other-than-God. He is like an ascetic who renounces world and devotes himself to God only for the sake of bodily repose, and in the hope that the world will come to him, because he knows that the Prophet ﷺ said, "Whoever cuts himself from everything for God, God will provide for him from whence he does not expect." And in another hadith, "Whoever directs all his intention towards the hereafter, God will ease his affair, put wealth in his heart, and make the herebelow grovel at his feet."

Or he is like one who renounces the world because he wants other people's esteem, honor, and recognition, or to be granted miracles, or to win the maidens and palaces of Paradise. In reality, such a person only travels from one creation to another, like a donkey at the mill, walking day and night but always ending up back where he started. The one whose aspiration is focused on selfish interests is like this donkey. He plods on, never leaving his location but imagining that he has traveled long distances in pursuit of his aims, getting nowhere despite all his toil.

Shaykh Abū al-Ḥasan ﷺ said, "Stay by one door, without hoping that other doors may be opened for you, though they will be. Submit yourself to only one Master, without hoping that

303 See Ibn ʿAjība's commentary on the 42nd aphorism of al-Iskandarī in *Īqāẓ al-himam*.

others may become subservient to you, though they will. God says: **Naught is there, but that its treasuries lie with Us.**"[304]

Dear disciple, you must raise your aspiration to the supreme Sovereign. You must travel the vision of created things and seek to behold the Ruling King; you must travel from evidence and proof to firsthand eye-witnessing. This is the furthest goal and the ultimate end: **The ultimate end is unto thy Lord.**[305]

Do not travel from one creature to another by sacrificing one self-interest for the sake of another, lest you be like the mill-donkey that always ends up back where it started. The comparison between this kind of person and the donkey is made in order to show his stupidity and small-mindedness. If he had God-given understanding, he would leave behind his self-interests and caprices and travel towards his Lord's presence. Dear disciple, do not leave one created world for another, but leave this created world for the One who created it, because the ultimate end is to your Lord.

To travel to your Lord, you require three things. The first is to focus your aspiration upon Him and no other, so when He looks in your heart, he finds no other beloved there but Him. The second is to fulfill your duties and abandon self-interest. The third is always to seek refuge with Him, ask His help, rely on Him, and surrender to whatever fate He decrees for you.

Shaykh Abū al-Ḥasan ﷺ said, "When four things are found in someone, the creatures need him while he does not need them: Love for God, enrichment in God, sincerity, and certainty: sincerity in worship, and certainty in the laws of Lordship. **And who is fairer in judgment than God, for a people who are certain?**"[306]

✵

The Junction of the Two Seas

When God wanted to show His Confidant, Sayyidunā Mūsā ﷺ, the truths of His almighty power, He commanded him to travel (*siyāḥa*) in the direction of the junction of the two seas, which is the isthmus between the two opposites. This story of his wandering on the horizons is explained in the commentaries on the Qur'ān, at least from an exoteric point of view. What we are interested in here is the *siyāḥa* of the soul through the levels of the heart.

So the Mūsā-heart set out, accompanied by the servant-soul, carrying the fish of caprice, with the intention of meeting the Khiḍr-spirit. Thus, the heart's accompaniment of the soul is purely for the sake of wayfaring, for the fields of the soul are where the heart's journey takes place, and the heart cannot travel any road but the road of the soul, as the *Ḥikam* says: "If it were not for the fields of the soul, the journey of the wayfarers would not become realized; for there is no distance

306 Q Mā'ida 5:50.

between you and Him that your journey must traverse, and there is no gap between you and Him that would be bridged by your arrival." [307]

So there is no distance between you and Him; **He is closer to you than your own jugular vein.** [308] Your journey is from you to yourself; from your senses to what is beyond them; from your earth to your heaven; from the illusion of your existence to your Creator who formed you.

The journey then is a metaphor for surmounting the obstacles of the soul and traversing the levels of the heart to attain knowledge of its different states and self-disclosures. On this journey, the disciple draws strength from the power of caprice and imagination, even if he is not aware of it. This is why God commanded the Confidant ﷺ to take the fish in the basket, and he made its loss, symbolizing the loss of caprice, the sign of his arrival at the junction of the two seas.

The fishes of Yūnus (Jonah, Dhū al-Nūn) and Sayyidunā Mūsā were of the same species. The fish symbolizes one of the pillars of the lower triangle by which God's Prophet Yūnus b. Matā ﷺ was tested. God tested him with the darkness of night, the ocean, and the belly of the fish.

So when the Mūsā-heart and the servant-soul reached the immolation stone, and the Confidant went to sleep there, the soul sprayed the fish with the water of life, and the station of life

307 See the 244th aphorism of al-Iskandarī.
308 Q Qāf 50:16.

was instilled in it, so it dove into the ocean of realities, sketching out the talisman of the meeting with the spirit as it went.

Ibn ʿAjība says:

The fish became a guide and an indicator for Sayyidunā Mūsā ﷺ only after its death and after being separated from him. Then it was revived with a special form of life when the water of life was sprinkled upon it. The same applies for the gnostic: it is only after dying to his sensory perceptions, transcending the obstacles of his soul, annihilating his mortal human nature, and subsisting through his Lord, that he can become a guide to God and a leader who is emulated. Then his spirit is revived through witnessing his Lord's magnificence, and he becomes a leader and a guide to Him. Extraordinary things appear at his hands, as happened with the fish when the flow of the water was held back from it so that it became like an arch, which was a divine miracle. The states of Khiḍr also alluded to this, and the fish was like a manifestation of his state in this story. [309]

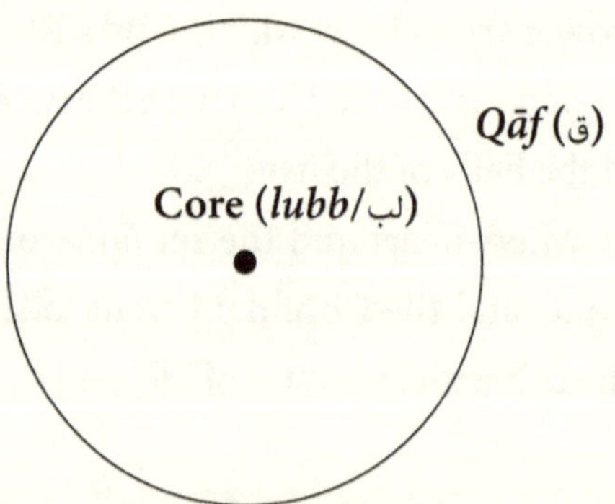

309 See Ibn ʿAjība's commentary on Q Kahf 18:60–82 in *Al-Baḥr al-madīd.*

Qāf + *lubb (core)* = *qalb* (heart)
Qāf is the soul; *lubb* is the spirit

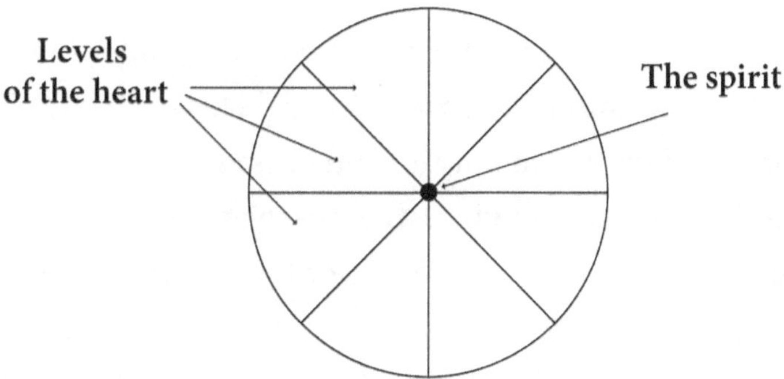

So this is the way of the *siyāḥa* of the soul through the levels of heart to reach the spirit. This is why it has been said that he who knows himself, knows his Lord. The *siyāḥa* of the soul is a journey to God. He who travels towards God will reach God; as for the one who travels with God, his journey has no end.

This journey, however, is reserved for the one who has found the red sulfur, the Shaykh who has arrived and can lead others to their arrival. This Shaykh is the **Blessed Olive Tree, neither of the east nor of the west.** [310] As for those who are not destined to find one, they must take up the *siyāḥa* of the physical world, which is to hold fast to the Sunna, fulfill one's obligations, and avoid misdeeds and missteps, in the hope that they may be accepted in the register of the true wayfaring men and women.

310 Q Nūr 24:35.

✪

The meaning of, "The wandering of my community is jihad in God's cause"

Abū Umāma ﷺ narrated that a certain man said, "Messenger of God, permit me to go wandering." He answered, "The wandering of my community is jihad in God's cause."[311]

The Prophet ﷺ was given the all-encompassing words (*jawāmiʿ al-kalim*), so that every word he spoke has seventy meanings, corresponding to the number of veils between God and creation. Every word he ﷺ utters contains the knowledge of the first and the last. How could it be otherwise, when as God tells us, **Nor does he speak out of caprice; it is naught but a revelation revealed.**[312]

The word "jihad", which is unfortunately too often limited to the meaning of "war," has made many young people of the Muslim community to fall into the notion that hatred for God's cause and disowning others is the pinnacle of the religion and the highest degree of faith. Yet God created this universe upon the foundation of love, and the principle of attraction is but one manifestation of this. A sublime understanding of the laws of the universe and the levels of the Name tells us that hate in reality is just one of the stations of love, and disowning is but one of the degrees of loyalty. Loyalty is the rule, and disowning is the exception; love is the rule, and hate is the exception. This is

311 Abū Dāwūd, *Sunan* #2130.
312 Q Najm 53:3-4.

why mercy precedes wrath in pre-eternity. Abū Hurayra narrated that the Prophet ﷺ said, "When God completed his creation, He wrote and placed above His Throne, 'My mercy prevails over My wrath.'"[313]

In fact, there are several types of jihad. Some of them are obligatory only for part of the Muslim community (*farḍ kifāya*), while others are obligatory on every individual (*farḍ al-ʿayn*), such as jihad against the lower self, which is the highest level of jihad known as "the greater jihad."

As for the quoted hadith, if we consider it at the station of spiritual excellence (*iḥsān*), it means that the real *siyāḥa* is the jihad of the disciple on God's path, the path of realization of the levels of the Supreme Name. It is the journey from the levels of the *Hāʾ* of Identity, to the *Lām* of Constriction, to the *Lām* of Gnosis, to the Cloud of the Lord, to the *Alif* of *tawḥīd*.

This *siyāḥa* is at the same time esoteric and exoteric, physical and spiritual. Through it, the disciple wanders in the worlds of his self, swimming in the deep cosmic realities of his Shaykh. The disciple becomes as the earth, which rotates on its axis, and at the same time floats in orbit around the sun, which is its origin and the secret held within it. Indeed, the center of the earth is nothing more than a miniature sun.

313 Bukhārī, *Ṣaḥīḥ* #7021.

Despite its state of stillness (*sukūn*), the sun **sails to its own resting place.** [314] As for earth, its movement is the expression of its desire to reach that state of stillness. The sun establishes itself upon the throne of love by becoming completely incinerated in the pre-eternal Beloved, whereas the earth seeks to burn up in the love of the center of its orbit. The closer it gets to the sun, the closer it gets to its annihilation, and the closer its hour comes.

The state of stillness only pertains to the Shaykh, because his saintly aspiration is extinguished in the One he desires, for He is his identity. As has been said, "if not for the mediator, there would be nothing to be mediated." As for the state of motion, it is on the part of the disciple seeking extinction in the mediator.

Stillness is thus the station of the Shaykh, while motion is the manifestation-site of the disciple. The one who becomes still through God knows Him, while the one who moves in Him limits and confines Him.

✪

The Disciple's Provision

The disciple must take provisions on his journey, in the form of some knowledge of the Sacred Law, for he must know the Sunna of the Beloved regarding travel, of which God says: **But**

---

314 Q Yāsīn 36:38.

it is not for the believers all to go forth. And why should not a party from each group go forth to acquire knowledge of religion, and to warn their people when they return to them, that haply they will beware?[315]

Know that *siyāḥa* is founded on firm resolve, not religious dispensations. For the seeker must discipline his soul and cultivate firm resolve without showing enmity toward it or imposing excessive hardship upon it; for anyone who tries to make the religion harder upon himself will surely be defeated by it. He must therefore treat the soul like the sea: when it is stormy and the waves are fierce, he should cling to his obligations; when it is calm and tranquil, he should engage in supererogatory devotions without going so far as to become a monk.

One aspect of the Law of which the wanderer must not be ignorant are the rules of the dry ablution (*tayammum*), water, combining and shortening prayers, wiping over socks, and other aspects of travel which have a bearing on worship and alter its rules. He must endeavor to learn this according to the school of our Imam Mālik ﷺ.

He should also be aware that every branch of the Sacred Law has a root in spiritual realization, and that every word, deed, and tacit approval of the Chosen Prophet ﷺ—and what is more, every breath he took, every whispered remark he made, and everything he came into contact with—was a matter of spiritual realization.

315 Q Tawba 9:122.

✸

Regarding the Dry Ablution (*tayammum*)

Tayammum is a dry ablution consisting of rubbing the face and hands with a proper intention. It is allowed in seven situations: (1) when not having enough water, (2) when unable to use water, (3) when fearing that water will cause or exacerbate illness or slow recovery, (4) when one's animal will otherwise go thirsty, (5) when one fears that valuable property will be ruined if water is used, (6) when there is not enough time to use water before the prayer is missed, and (7) when there is water nearby but one does not have any way of getting it. Those in any of these situations may do *tayammum* whether they are travelling or at home, even if the journey involves something sinful. A single *tayammum* may be done for one obligatory prayer on its own, or for a voluntary prayer done immediately after it, but not for two obligatory prayers done back-to-back, or for a voluntary prayer done before an obligatory one.

Shaykh al-ʿAlawī said of this in *al-Minaḥ al-quddūsiyya*, his mystical commentary on the Sacred Law:

The one who purifies himself with a dry ablution should not seek the prayer of union, but only the prayer of separation, for he is separated by the impurity of temporality, which has not truly been lifted from his gaze. For he is constrained by its limits, unlike the one who purifies himself with nondelimited water (*māʾ muṭlaq*), whose purification is as nondelimited as the water itself, while the other's purification is delimited by the delimitations of earth. Water symbolizes the suprasensory realm, while earth symbolizes the sensory realm; and what a difference there is between one who purifies himself with the sensorial, and one who purifies himself with the suprasensorial! The sensorial cannot purify the physical. The one who uses water knows God through God, while the one who uses earth knows God through other-than-God. What a difference between the one who seeks proofs for Him, and the one for whom He is the Proof![316]

The example we have given of *tayammum* may serve to stand in for all other matters of worship, social interaction, and rulings, so that the intention of the Law is recognized. There is a vast difference between applying the Law with understanding and applying it without understanding. Practice rooted in knowledge and understanding of the Lawgiver's intent contains sweetness and bliss known only to those who experience it. The soul, moreover, finds it easy to adhere to this with consistency.

If you desire to know more, consult the books of the Sufis who examined the esoteric meaning of the Law such as *al-Minah al-quddūsiyya*, authored by our shaykh Sīdī Aḥmad b. ʿAlīwa al-Mustaghānamī (d. 1934), may God sanctify his spirit.

---

316 ʿAlawī, *al-Minah al-quddūsiyya* p. 127.

✪

The Proper Courtesy of *Siyāḥa*

Siyāḥa is fundamentally a matter of beautiful character, which is the celestial mount that carries the wayfarer to the ultimate destination. Upon its back, he rapidly traverses stations that would take others years to get through. As for the one who displays ugly character toward his brethren or toward the public by repaying one ill turn with another, his *siyāḥa* will be fruitless, and such a person must renew his repentance. After all, the purpose of *siyāḥa* is to bear abuse and be patient with one's brethren and with the public, and this can only be achieved by means of beautiful character. Here are some noble hadiths to illustrate the virtue and merit of this in the eyes of the Lord:

Jābir related that God's Messenger ﷺ said, "The dearest of you to me, and the nearest on the Day of Resurrection, will be those with the most beautiful character. The most detestable of you to me, and the furthest on the Day of Resurrection, will be the chatterers, the braggarts, and the proud."[317]

Abū Hurayra related that God's Messenger ﷺ said, "The dearest of you to me are those with the most beautiful character, those who are easygoing and get on well with others. The most detestable of you to me are those who spread gossip, sow discord among those who love one another, and seek out the faults of innocent people."[318]

317 Tirmidhī, *Jāmiʿ* 1937#.
318 Ṭabarānī, *Awsaṭ* #837.

Anas related that God's Messenger ﷺ said, "The person with the most perfect faith is the one with the most beautiful character. Beautiful character is on the level of fasting and praying."[319]

Abū Hurayra related that God's Messenger ﷺ said, "The believers with the most perfect faith are those with the most beautiful character. The best of you are those who are kindest to women."[320]

Abū Hurayra related that God's Messenger ﷺ was asked what thing is most responsible for people entering Paradise, and replied, "Reverence of God and beauty of character." Then he was asked what thing is most responsible for people entering Hell, and replied, "The mouth and the loins."[321]

Usāma b. Sharīk related that some Bedouins asked God's Messenger ﷺ about a number of harmless things, until finally he said, "Servants of God! God has lifted all harm, except for the one who dares to impute the honor of his fellow Muslim unjustly. That is what harms and ruins." They said, "May we use medicine, Messenger of God?" He replied, "Yes, do so, for God has made a cure for every ailment, except one: old age." They said, "Messenger of God, what is the best gift a person has ever been given?" He replied, "Beautiful character."[322]

---

319 *Kashf al-astār* #35.
320 Tirmidhī, *Jāmiʿ* #1078.
321 Tirmidhī, *Jāmiʿ* #2004.
322 Ḥākim, *Mustadrak*.

'Abd Allāh b. Mas'ūd related that God's Messenger ﷺ said, "Shall I not tell you of the one who is saved from Hell? It is the one who is easygoing and pleasant with his relatives."[323]

Proper etiquette, then, is one aspect of beautiful character, and courtesy is the spirit of Sufism, to the extent that is has been said that the one who is more courteous than you is a better Sufi than you. It has also been said that your worship should be like salt [which adds taste to the food], your courtesy like refined flour. The reason these proverbs exist is that the Sufis perceive the merit and blessing of proper etiquette. It has several facets: there is courtesy with God, courtesy with the mediator, courtesy with one's brethren, and courtesy with the public.

Courtesy with God during *siyāḥa* is to rely on Him and throw oneself down before His mercy, like a feather floating in the breeze of His omnipotence. It is to be ascetic, and content oneself with the bare minimum of worldly comforts.

Courtesy with the mediator is to be constantly aware of its reality, so that it divests you of your own existence and you do not see yourself, but only your Shaykh in everything significant you do, as defined by the standards of the Sacred Law and esoteric Reality. For it is through him that you connect with the Light of God's Messenger ﷺ. He is both the door and the door-keeper, so throw yourself into the lap of his innermost secret.

Courtesy with one's brethren is to be patient and overlook flaws, and indeed to revere the secrets and Lights hidden within

323 Tirmidhī, *Jāmi'* #2488.

them. They are but attributes of divine self-disclosure, so revere them. It is also to seek their counsel, for blessing lies in consulting them. The Lord encouraged His Messenger to consult his Companions, even though in reality he ※ did not need to do so: **Then [it was] by a mercy from God that thou wert gentle with them. Hadst thou been severe [and] hard-hearted they would have scattered from about thee. So pardon them, ask forgiveness for them, and consult them in affairs. And when thou art resolved, trust in God; truly God loves those who trust.** [324]

It is also to prefer others over oneself, as God says: **They prefer others over themselves, even if they be impoverished. And whosoever is shielded from the avarice of his soul, it is they who shall prosper.** [325]

Finally, courtesy with the public means to pray that they be guided and given God's grace, and to view them through the eye of realization. One of the gnostics said, "View yourself through the eye of the Law, and others through the eye of esoteric Reality." The eye of Reality is the eye of Beauty, through which you see all things in the Light of God's mercy. Treat them with mercy, compassion, and gentleness, as God's Messenger ※ said, "The prayer God loves the most is when His servant says, 'Dear God, have mercy on the community of Muḥammad, all of them.'"

---

324 Q Āl ʿImrān 3:159.
325 Q Ḥashr 59:9.

6.

The Spiritual Retreat (*khalwa*)

In the Arabic language:

The word *khalwa* means a place of solitude where a Sufi goes to engage in worship. [326]

In the Terminology of the Karkariya Order:

It is to dwell in the tomb of life, in order to disengage from the sensory realm and journey to the world of pure meaning, while carrying the provision of the Name and practicing complete detachment, so that you may enter into the heart and keep the company of the Lord, till the veil is parted and inner vision is sharpened with the metal of eternity.

In the Holy Qur'ān:

God says: **So her Lord accepted her with a beautiful acceptance, and made her to grow in a beautiful way, and placed her under the care of Zachariah. Whenever Zachariah entered upon her in the sanctuary he found provision with her. He**

326 *Al-Muʿjam al-ʿarabī al-asāsī*, p. 422.

said, "Mary, whence comes this unto thee?" She said, "It is from God. Truly God provides for whomsoever He will without reckoning." [327]

God says: **And We appointed for Moses thirty nights, and We completed them with ten [more]; thus was completed the appointed term of his Lord: forty nights. And Moses said unto his brother, Aaron, "Take my place among my people, set matters aright, and follow not the way of those who work corruption."** [328]

God says: **Dost thou reckon that the Companions of the Cave and the Inscription are a marvel among Our signs? When the youths took refuge in the cave, they said, "Our Lord! Grant us mercy from Thy Presence, and make us incline to sound judgment concerning our affair."** [329]

God says: **So he came forth from the sanctuary unto his people, and signaled to them that they should glorify morning and evening.** [330]

In the Noble Hadith:

'Ā'isha ﷺ related: "The first revelation given to God's Messenger ﷺ was in the form of true dreams in his sleep, which were all as bright and clear as the rising sun. He used to go to Ḥirā' Cave and spend many nights there in worship, taking pro-

327   Q Āl 'Imrān 3:37.
328   Q A'rāf 7:142.
329   Q Kahf 18:9-10.
330   Q Maryam 19:11.

visions with him, and then return to Khadīja for more. This went on until suddenly the truth descended upon him while he was in Ḥirā'. The angel came to him there and told him, 'Recite!' The Prophet ﷺ replied, 'I am not a reciter.'"

[The Prophet ﷺ recalled:] "The angel took hold of me and embraced me until I could not no longer bear it, then released me and said, 'Recite!' I replied, 'I am not a reciter.' He took hold of me a second time and embraced me until I could no longer bear it, then released me and said, 'Recite!' I replied, 'I am not a reciter.' He took hold of me a third time and embraced me until I could no longer bear it, then released me and said, **Recite in the Name of thy Lord Who created, created man from a blood clot. Recite! Thy Lord is most noble, Who taught by the Pen, taught man that which he knew not."** [331]

['Ā'isha continued:] "Then he returned home with the Inspiration, trembling with terror. He went in to Khadīja and said, "Cover me! Cover me!" She covered him till his fear was over, and then he said, 'Khadīja, what is wrong with me?' He told her everything that had happened and said, 'I fear for myself.' Khadīja said, 'Never! Rejoice, for by God, God would never disgrace you. You keep good relations with your kin, speak the truth, help the poor and the destitute, serve your guests generously, and assist righteous causes.' Khadīja then accompanied him to her cousin Waraqa, who had become a Christian during the pre-Islamic era and used to write the Gospels in Arabic. He

---

331 Q 'Alaq 96:1-5.

was an old man and had lost his eyesight. Khadīja said to him, 'Cousin! Listen to your nephew's story.' Waraqa asked, 'Nephew, what have you seen?' The Prophet ﷺ described what he had seen. Waraqa said, 'This is the same *Nomos* that was sent down to Moses. I wish I were young and could live to see the day when your people drive you out.' God's Messenger ﷺ asked, 'Will they drive me out?' Waraqa replied, 'Yes. Never did a man bring the like of what you have brought, but that he was treated with hostility. If I should remain alive till your day comes, I will lend you all my support.' But Waraqa died shortly afterwards, and the Inspiration also paused for a while. [332]

Ibn Masʿūd related that the Messenger of God ﷺ, the Truthful Honest One, said, "The matter of the creation of a human being is put together in the womb of the mother in forty days, and then becomes a clot for a similar period, and then a piece of flesh for a similar period. Then God sends an angel who is commanded to write four things, and told: 'Write down his deeds, his provision, his life-span, and whether he is felicitous or wretched.' Then the spirit is breathed into him. Thus, a man may do good deeds till there is only a cubit between him and Paradise, but then his fate catches up with him and he does the deeds of the Hell-bound. And likewise, a man may do evil deeds till there is only a cubit between him and Hell, but then his fate catches up with him and he does the deeds of the Heaven-bound." [333]

332 Bukhārī, *Ṣaḥīḥ* #3.
333 Bukhārī, *Ṣaḥīḥ* #2988.

Anas b. Malik reported that God's Messenger ﷺ said: "Spend your lives in the pursuit of the good, and expose yourselves to the breezes of God's mercy; for God sends breezes of His mercy upon whomever of His servants He wishes. Ask God to cover you when you are uncovered, and to grant safety to those in your care."[334]

Abū Ayyūb al-Anṣārī reported that God's Messenger ﷺ said, "He who devotes forty days to God will have springs of wisdom flow forth from his tongue."

✦

And We Appointed for Moses

God says, **And We appointed for Moses thirty nights, and We completed them with ten [more]; thus was completed the appointed term of his Lord: forty nights. And Moses said unto his brother, Aaron, "Take my place among my people, set matters aright, and follow not the way of those who work corruption."**[335]

When God wants to honor one of His servants, He arranges an appointment for them to rid them of the stain of heedlessness, and ignite in their hearts the passion of repentance, contrition, and humility. The turbidities of separation are burned

334 Bayhaqī, *Shuʿab* #1081.
335 Q Aʿrāf 7:142.

away by the flames of passion and love, and the veils of the Acts and Attributes become finer.

This appointment is the hidden source of the Name, the door of mystical truth. It is called *al-Dahr*, the Aeon, which is both a Name and an Attribute. Abū Hurayra narrated that Messenger of God ﷺ said: "God says, 'The children of Adam inveigh against the Aeon, but I am the Aeon; in My hand is the night and the day.'" [336]

The tradition of the Appointment was established so that your primordial dot may be written, and the secret of your vicegerency may be made plain. As for God, He is hallowed beyond time and space. He has no beginning or end; nothing precedes Him or succeeds Him.

How, then, could our Lord come to an appointment, when He is the Aeon Itself? In reality, every soul has a moment of unveiling and manifestation, a time of awe and presence, according to what was destined for it in pre-eternity. This is when the soil of his being rises, and the tree of divine contentment and expansion sprouts from it, bearing the fruits of the wonders of beauty and perfection. He rises up in passionate rapture to the heaven of divine Oneness, and his innermost secret floats in the uncreated reality of the divine Ipseity, and he comes to naught between contraction and expansion, beauty and majesty.

336 Bukhārī, *Ṣaḥīḥ* #5742.

Sayyidunā Ibn al-Fāriḍ (may God sanctify his secret) said of this:

When the Appointment drew near
For my all-enveloping union,

My mountain was rendered unto dust
In awe of the Self-Discloser.

Then was unveiled a hidden secret
That only one such as I could perceive:

Death in Him is my life,
And in my life is my death.

I am the tormented pauper,
Have pity on my wretched state!

God's promise to His servant is noble and great. His appointment comes during the hour of love, and His meeting place is on the passionate mountain of Ṭūr, where the lovers gather in the holy presence of the Only.

Come, dear disciple, to Our appointment without your own being; come when no remnant of yourself remains in you, when you are annihilated in Our presence, subsisting by Our holiness, beholding Us and Our awesome Majesty and tender Beauty, your name annihilated in Ours, your trace in Ours, your whole and your every part belonging to Me. It is then that you will find Me. Majesty will show you the Path, and Beauty will light your way. You will find Me waiting for you, yearning for you even more than you yearned for Me, for you are but a part of Me, while I am your All.

Sayyidunā Abū Yazīd al-Bisṭāmī said, "I called Abū Yazīd to God, but he refused, so I left him and went to God myself."

And Sayyidunā Ibn ʿArabī (may God sanctify his secret) said:

I had loved ones who gave me the advice
That all the folk of love and gnosis give:

They advised me to invoke God at all times,
And the Invoked annihilated them from
the presence of invocation;

Then, when they became extinct to all that exists,
And took comfort in nothing but the Night of Power,

The unity of the Folk became a holy Odd,
And the Odd delivered its discourse to Itself.

✦

Separation (*faṣl*) and Union (*waṣl*)

The secret of gnosis (*maʿrifa*) is an isthmus between a thing and its shadow, negation and affirmation, presence and absence, yes and no. The human being is a gathering-place of opposites, and hence a disclosure-site of separation and union. God says, **Truly We created man in the most beautiful stature, then We cast him to the lowest of the low.** [337] The **most beautiful stature** is pure union, and the **lowest of the low** is pure separation. Separation is the manifestation-site of the lower state, union of the upper state. Each necessitates the other, and there is a dialectical relationship between them, such that union can only come after separation, and there is no separation without union.

Now God breathed His spirit into man, and then tested him with a lower soul, and giving each of them their own powers and allies. Ibn ʿAṭāʾ Allāh says in one of his aphorisms: "Light is the ally of the heart, just as darkness the ally of the lower soul. When God wishes to assist His servant, He gives him allies of Light and blocks the influx of darkness and alterity." [338]

God says: **God is the Protector of those who believe. He brings them out of the darkness into the Light. As for those who disbelieve, their protectors are the false idols, bringing**

---

337 Q Tīn 95:4-5.
338 See the 56th aphorism of al-Iskandarī.

them out of the Light into the darkness. They are the inhabitants of the Fire, abiding therein. [339]

So Light is the secret of union, the manifestation-site of the saintly protection that God lends His servant. As for darkness, it is the station of separation, of the false idol and its allies.

Ḥudhayfa related that God's Messenger said, "Temptations are presented to the heart as a reed mat is woven, strip by strip. The heart that absorbs these [temptations] is marked with a black dot, while the heart that rejects them is marked by a white dot. Accordingly, there are two types of hearts: one that is white like as a white stone. It is unharmed by turmoil or temptation so long as the heavens and the earth remain. The other is dark and dusty like a turbid vessel. It neither recognizes what is good, nor rejects what is reprehensible, but judging all based on its caprice." [340]

So each luminous mark leads closer to a union of sanctity between the Lord and His servant. If the Light continues to grow without interruption, it will result in a pure and illuminated heart touched by the Real. For just as the Name the All-Merciful ascends the throne, so the Name *Allāh* ascends the believer's heart.

On the contrary, each black mark leads to separation and carries the servant farther from the Lord. If this black mark continues to grow, it will lead to the growth of the demonic tree of Zaqqūm, whose fruits are like the heads of demons.

339 Q Baqara 2:257.
340 Muslim, *Ṣaḥīḥ* #211.

There is allusion to this in God's words:

When Saul set out with the hosts he said, "Truly God will try you with a river. Whosoever drinks from it is not of me, and whosoever tastes not of it is of me—save one who scoops out a handful." But they drank from it, save a few among them. So when he crossed it, he and those who believed with him, they said, "We have no power today against Goliath and his hosts." Those who deemed they would meet their Lord said, "How many a small company have overcome a large company by God's Leave! And God is with the patient." And when they went forth against Goliath and his hosts they said, "Our Lord, pour patience upon us, make firm our steps, and help us against the disbelieving people." And they routed them, by God's Leave, and David slew Goliath, and God gave him sovereignty and wisdom, and taught him of what He wills. And were it not for God's repelling people, some by means of others, the earth would have been corrupted. But God is Possessed of Bounty for the worlds. [341]

Before explaining those verses, I will lay down a general rule; if you hold to it and apply it, you will gain access to an understanding of God's Book, and you will be able to dive into its esoteric meanings and glean its most precious secrets.

This rule is this: "Do not come out of your grave." That is, remain within your body, because within you is gathered all the universe and its meanings, and the divine Names and their

---

341 Q Baqara 2:249-251.

secrets. You are the manifestation-site of the opposites, the isthmus of the two seas, the master of this world and the next. So do not think that you are an insignificant tiny being, for the macrocosm is contained within you.

Now let us proceed:

When the Saul-spirit **set out** (*faṣala*) with his hosts, God tempted them with the **river** of the base desires of separation (*faṣl*). The spirit said to the hosts, **Truly God will try you with a river. Whosoever drinks from it is not of me**; that is, not from the world of the spirit and unveiling; **and whosoever tastes not of it is of me**; that is, from My world, and he will receive My Lights and disclosures; **one who scoops out a handful**, according to what is permitted by wisdom and the principle of gradualness.

But they drank from it, namely those who supported the soul and were destined for separation because of the powerful correspondence between them and it; for it was the river of corporeal nature; **save a few among them**, namely the intellect, the heart, and the senses that were subordinate to them.

So they crossed the valley of the false idol and its darkness, and the spirit breathed certitude into them, and they said, **"How many a small company have overcome a large company by God's Leave! And God is with the patient." And when they went forth against Goliath**, namely the evil-enjoining soul, and his hosts, **they said, "Our Lord, pour patience upon us**, the patience of the gnostics, **make firm our steps** in the registry of the righteous, **and help us against the disbelieving people." And they routed them, by God's Leave, and the David of the intellect slew the sensory passion of the Goliath of the soul and took hold of its reins, and so was made sovereign of his corporeal kingdom by the secret of the spiritual heaven. Then the heart ruled the hosts of the limbs and the senses, and attained knowledge of the secret of its essence through its essence.

✤

Unification (*al-jam'*)

In the Arabic language:
The word *jam'* means for something that has been taken apart to be put back together. [342]

In the Terminology of the Karkariya Order:
It is the wellspring of the universal Qur'ānic reality that subsists through the loci of existence and nonexistence, beyond all expression, allusion, or description, transcending the separations of duality, folding up all notions of proximity and spatiality, so that extinction is extinguished and the Real is witnessed without creation.

Jam' means for the part to be added to the all, the branch joined to the root, so that the Real is beheld through the Real,

---

342   *Al-Mu'jam al-'arabī al-asāsī* p. 360.

and the disclosures of the beauty of the Attributes and Names are witnessed as they flow through the bases of the boughs of separation. Only then will you see the one flowing in all the numbers, the *Alif* flowing through all the letters. Only then will you see Him in everything, and all images will be extinguished in its own subsistence (*baqā'*), vanishing into the root its own existence, so that the expanded universe is stitched back together.

God says: **Have those who disbelieve not considered that the heavens and the earth were stitched together, and We rent them asunder? And We made every living thing from water. Will they not, then, believe?** [343]

That is, those who conceal (lit. *kufr*) reality itself, namely the first determination of the Essence; **have they not considered that the heavens** of the spirit **and the earth** of the body were a **stitched-up** primordial mass free of any determination or perspective, and **then We rent them asunder** by the Unity that manifests the illusory realm of multiplicity? **And We made from the water** of divinity **every living thing**, through the just balance of the Names, which gives every named thing its effective relation.

The station of unification, then, is one of the founding principles of spiritual training for the Sufis. If a person has no unification, he has no witnessing; and if he has no witnessing, he has no gnosis.

343 Q Anbiyā' 21:30.

Consequently, the return of the expanded seven heavens, the seven earths, the Footstool and the Throne to their original stitched-up state is one of the founding principles of our Way. Through it, the disciple will see the role of the one throughout all the numbers, and thereby witness the acts of God through the acts of His servants, so that all the actions will be seen as coming from Him. With this, he will witness all alterities through God, and the Name and its properties will become manifest to him while the form and its illusions will disappear. The receptacles will speak with the tongue of Eternity, and unity will be contemplated in the heart of multiplicity. The insight of the spirit will be drawn to the vision of eternal Beauty. He will then come to recognize that multiplicity has no existence in and of itself, but is merely an ephemeral shadow. He will observe all things as existing through the real Essence, not through themselves. The perceptions of other-than-God will be extinguished, and the disciple will disappear into the ocean of Ipseity.

✪

The Folding-Up (*al-ṭayy*)

In the Arabic language:
The verb *ṭawā* means "to fold something over itself." [344]

344 *Al-Muʿjam al-ʿarabī al-asāsī* p. 387.

In the Terminology of the Karkariya Order:

It is to fold the soul's written book of outward dispositions into the spirit's scroll of eye-witnessed realities. God says: **That Day We shall roll up the sky like the rolling up of scrolls of the written book. As We began the first creation, so shall We bring it back—a promise binding upon Us. Surely We shall do it.**[345]

God says: **That Day We shall roll up the sky,** i.e., on the **Day** when mankind stands at plane of resurrection, and the skies are folded and rolled up **like the rolling of scrolls of the written book;** i.e., the way the scribe folds the page in half to write on it; or the way a page is rolled up to preserve what has already been written on it.

Abū Ja'far read this verse with the verb in the passive voice: **That Day the sky shall be rolled up.** This refers to the erasure of the sky's form and the rolling-up of its stars, sun, and moon. The primary meaning of *ṭayy* is "to roll up", the opposite of "to unroll." Ḥafṣ reads the word *kitāb* (**written book**) as *kutub* in the plural; that is, like folding a page for the many meanings written thereon, or like rolling them up to protect them.[346]

The disciple too must **fold up** the **written book** of his egoic illusions, and forget what he knew and what he knew not. He must **fold it all into** the Lord's **scroll** of luminous and pure meaning. For the heaven of divine secrets **shall not be opened,** nor will he **enter** the garden of pure meanings and gnostic sciences, until **the camel** of his soul **passes through the needle's**

345 Q Anbiyā' 21:104.
346 *Al-Baḥr al-madīd* vol. 4 p. 387.

eye of his spirit. God says: **Truly those who deny Our signs and wax arrogant against them, the gates of Heaven shall not be opened for them, nor shall they enter the Garden till the camel passes through the needle's eye. Thus do We recompense the guilty!**[347]

Sīdī Aḥmad al-ʿAlawī (may God sanctify his secret) says:

Invoke the Supreme Name, and fold up the cosmos to succeed;
Dive into the pre-eternal ocean, for that is the Ocean of God.

Dive into the ocean of Lights, the ocean
of pure meanings and secrets;
Annihilate this illusory world, and your heart
will reach the One it desires.

The folding-up is divided into three categories: the folding-up of time, the folding-up of place, and the folding-up of time and space together. The folding-up of place is terrestrial, whereas the folding-up of time is temporal. They are distinct from the folding-up that is mentioned in some Sufi books, for the latter describe a sensory folding, while we are concerned with a suprasensory folding.

The corporeal earth is the locus of the imprinting of the divine Names, while aeonic-time (*al-zamān al-dayhūrī*) is the locus of the imprinting of the divine Attributes. When the dis-

347 Q Aʿrāf 7:40.

ciple folds up the Attribute in the Name, and then the Name in the Named, the oneness of the Real will be disclosed to him, and the star of universal existence will appear him. Then the pillars of his soul will swell, and the earth of this existence will begin to shake, and it will give up the treasures of its gnostic sciences and reveal its secrets. The books of the soul will be folded within the scroll of the spirit, and the disciple will return to his origin. His hidden part will become manifest to him, and his secrets will disclose themselves to him, and then he will understand the meaning of, "God was, and there was nothing with Him."

Sīdī ʿAbd al-Raḥmān al-Shāghūrī ✿ (d. 2004) says:

The veils of separation were lifted,
and the Lights of the source appeared,

Disclosing themselves beyond space,
so behold them, O Sufis!

I am the mirror of my Beloved;
O my spirit, delight in His love!

O my soul, be absent from all but Him,
and discard all base things.

Ever since these visions began,
I have been bowing and prostrating,

Thanking and praising Him
for folding me up in His ipseity.

Ibn 'Aṭā' Allāh al-Iskandarī says in one of his aphorisms: "The real folding-up is to fold the dimensions of the herebelow and to behold the hereafter as being closer to you than your own self." [348] This is the kind of folding-up desired from you: that your soul and its desires, passions, and needs are folded up for you, so that you become detached from the world. Then the world itself and its baubles and illusions are folded up from you, and you behold how the hereafter is closer to you than your own self. Then the hereafter itself and all its gardens, palaces, and maidens are folded up from you, and there is nothing left but you and your Lord.

✧

Beauty (*al-jamāl*)

In the Arabic language:

Jamāl is an attribute perceived in things that instills joy or a feeling of order and harmony in the soul. It is one of the three conceptual standards by which the values of things are judged: beauty, truth, and goodness. [349]

---

348 See the 82nd aphorism of al-Iskandarī.
349 *Al-Mu'jam al-'arabī al-asāsī* p. 264.

In the Terminology of the Karkariya Order:

Beauty is the disclosure of the splendor of the Essence through the manifestation of the Names and Attributes. It is the illumination of the Light of the Beloved upon the servant's heart, until he sees nothing in existence but the Beauty of God, and his every sight, hearing, motion, and stillness are through Him. At that point, the property of ugliness no longer exists except in a relative sense, as God says: **Say, "All is from God." What is with these people that they scarcely understand any tiding?** [350]

When the soul comes to naught in the presence of the Real, the cosmos adorns itself with the Light of divine Beauty. It then becomes clear that ugliness is nothing but a relative property, and that what is ugly to one beholder is the height of beauty to another. At this stage of perception, everything is seen as coming from God. Beauty is thus the manifestation-site of mercy and clemency, and it is through the grace of this mercy that the divine Beauty flows, and is the cause of all creation. It is the substance of beauty and the essence of perfection.

Beauty is divided into two sorts:

Absolute beauty (*jamāl muṭlaq*)

Absolute beauty is the beauty of God represented in His perfection, His hidden secret that in reality is what is sought by

---

350 Q Nisā' 4:78.

every seeker of divine love. It was through this beauty that man became the vicegerent of God on His earth, for he was created upon the beauty of the All-Merciful.

To this effect, Imam al-Bukhārī narrates on the authority of Abū Hurayra that the Prophet ﷺ said, "God created Adam in His image, sixty cubits tall. When He created him, He said 'Go and greet those angels sitting over there, and listen to how they reply to you, for that will be your greeting and the greeting of your progeny.' So Adam said, 'Peace be upon you', and they replied, 'And upon you be peace and God's mercy', adding 'and God's mercy.' All those who enter Paradise will have the image of Adam. Ever since then, mankind has been diminishing in size." [351]

So perfect beauty is found in the Perfect Man (*al-insān al-kā-mil*), for he is the beauty of the knowledge of the Names, and the beauty of the eternal Attribute of God. God beholds His own attribute within His Essence, and manifests the Perfect Man through that luminous beholding, like a mirror in which He contemplates His own beauty.

The entire cosmos is therefore an expression of the absolute splendor through the attribute of beauty; and in reality, what appears ugly therein is also beautiful. All is beautiful, because all is the disclosure-site of the divine Beauty.

---

351 Bukhārī, *Ṣaḥīḥ* #5788.

He who views the universe in this way, and meditates on the beauty of the cosmos, will arrive at the Creator, because the universe is the manifestation of the Real. At this stage, what was ugly becomes beautiful. Passionate love for the beauty of a thing therefore leads to its Creator.

Qualified beauty (*al-jamāl al-muqayyad*)

Qualified beauty is the beauty of a thing through the qualification of its receptacle. If that thing were to disappear, the love for it would also disappear; and if that thing were to change, the degree of love for it would also change. This is because the thingness of each thing is but an ephemeral shadow, while absolute inner beauty persists forever without change, only becoming more intense as the mirror of the heart becomes cleaner so that it better reflects the divine Beauty. Upon beholding true beauty, the lover experiences true enrapturement in the beauty of the Real.

We can notice that there are different degrees of rapture, in accordance with the purity of the mirror of the heart. Some people see God's beauty before the beauty of things; others see the beauty of the thing before the beauty of God; others see both at the same time; and finally, there are those who see only the beauty of God, which is the highest level, though the others are not at fault.

Sīdī Ibn ʿAṭāʾ Allāh al-Iskandarī says, "The Real is not veiled; it is you who are veiled from seeing Him. For if anything were to veil Him, it would have to cover Him, which would be to limit His existence; and if something limits another thing, it overpowers it." [352]

Consequently, the only things that obstruct you from beholding His beauty are your own illusions. Leave yourself behind, and you will find Him closer to you than yourself, openly disclosed to you through His Light.

✪

And Moses Fell Down in a Swoon

In the Terminology of the Karkariya Order:
The term "swoon" (ṣaʿq) means to become extinguished from, by, and to yourself, so that your vision never swerves from your innermost secret, nor transgresses against the reality of your essence. May God reward Abū Madyan who said:

All the worlds were lifted from me,
And the Light of my heart shone forth.

What was hidden became manifest,
And I folded up all the universe.

My cups were served to me from me;
After my death, you see me alive.

352 See the 19ᵗʰ aphorism of al-Iskandarī.

God says: **And when Moses came to Our appointed meeting and his Lord spoke unto him, he said, "My Lord, show me, that I might look upon Thee." He said, "Thou shalt not see Me; but look upon the mountain: if it remains firm in its place, then thou wilt see Me." And when his Lord disclosed Himself to the mountain, He made it crumble to dust, and Moses fell down in a swoon. And when he recovered, he said, "Glory be to Thee! I turn unto Thee in repentance, and I am the first of the believers."** [353]

Moses came forth like a passionate lover; **Moses came** forth without **Moses**; **Moses came** forth with nothing remaining of himself for himself. Thousands of men have walked long distances but were remembered by no one, but the few steps **Moses** took will be studied by schoolchildren until the end of time: **And when Moses came...** [354]

At the time of **the appointed meeting,** the waves of his soul's inner thoughts fell still, and his hearing was purified from the limitations of the created letters, so that the Confidant experienced the reality of, "I become his hearing with which he hears." For the pre-eternal Word can only be heard by a pre-eternal hearing.

The Confidant yearned for the holiness of the Valley, where the flood of eternity drowned him in the ocean of pre-eternity, and the waters of beginninglessness carried him to the Valley of Ṭuwā, where he removed his shoes.

353 Q A'rāf 7:143.
354 Qushayrī, *Laṭā'if al-ishārāt* vol. 1 p. 564.

When the time of the **appointment** came and the hour of annihilation arrived, the pleasures of fulfilled loved washed over Moses and he heard the sweetness of the divine address. He vanished in awe of the Majesty, and rose with his innermost secret to the Lote-Tree of the lovers, transported by the beauty and the power of what he heard.

Then, when intoxication and ecstasy overcame him, he asked to see his Lord. The intoxicated one is beyond reproach, for the lightness of expansion rents the veil of shyness asunder, and the inebriation of wine tears down the wall of courtesy.

Sīdī Abū Madyan (may God sanctify his secret) says:

When we rejoice and our souls take flight,
And the wine of passion intoxicates us,

Do not blame the drunkard as long as he is drunk,
For religious accountability is lifted so long
as we are drunk to ourselves.

So he said, **show me**, asking to be graced with the beatific vision; but the glory of unification refused the request of separation, and so answered in the negative in the station of transcendence upon the Mount, just as it responded in the negative in the station of immanence when he asked to accompany Sayyidunā al-Khiḍr.

The reason the pre-eternal presence replied with **Thou shalt not** was that the request implied the attributes of duality and spatiality, which the realities of Oneness and the glory of God-hood repudiate.

But look upon the mountain, the spatial mediator; **if it remains firm in its place** after the disclosure, then so shall you. **Then He disclosed Himself to the mountain** through the shadow of a needle's eye of lordly wisdom; for had He lifted the veil so much as a fingertip, He would have burned away the entire realm of spatiality. Abū Mūsā reported that God's Messenger ﷺ said, "God does not sleep, and it is not befitting that He should sleep. He lowers the Scales and raises them. His veil is Light, and if He were to remove it, the glory of His Face would burn everything of His creation, as far as His gaze reaches." [355]

So when the lordship disclosed itself to the mountain, it flew up into the heaven of the realm of invincibility and crumbled to dust, and **Moses fell down in a swoon** in awe at this station. Imam Shushtarī ؓ said in a poem:

The creation is Yours, and the command is Yours;
What, then, am I but a shadow?

The veil is non-existent in Your presence,
Except through the secret letters of **look upon the mountain.**

You guided people to You and from You,
Your eternality expresses the beginningless mystery.

355 Ibn Mājah, *Sunan* #192.

You made Yourself known to this knower, through Yourself;
You are they, O life of the heart, O my hope!

Then the attentive care of pre-eternity was sent down, and it elected Moses for post-eternity. It breathed into him the realities of the Essence. When he woke up, Moses exclaimed God's transcendence beyond all temporality, saying, **Glory be to Thee!** Now sober, he remembered his drunken utterances and said, **I turn unto Thee in repentance, and I am the first of the believers.**

Sayyidunā Aḥmad b. ʿAjība (may God sanctify his secret) said:

The Sufis affirm the possibility of seeing God in this life as well as the hereafter. However, only the elite of the elite can attain it in this life. They call it witnessing (*shuhūd*) or eye-witnessing (*ʿayān*), and it can only occur after extinction (*fanāʾ*), and the extinction of extinction, after the lower soul is slain and its senses and forms are transcended. This can only come after refinement and training at the hands of a perfected Shaykh, who continues to guide the disciple through the stations and beyond his own soul and regard for its existence, until finally he tells him, "Here you are, and here is your Lord."

The Real discloses Himself to His servants through the secrets of pure meanings behind the cloak of vessels, which are the sensory aspects of created things. The secrets of pure meanings can only be manifested through the medium of vessels. Or we might say that the secrets of the Essence can only be manifested through the Lights of the Attributes, for if they appeared without any medium, all things would be burned up and anni-hilated, as the hadith says: "His veil is Light, and if He were to remove it, the glory of His Face would burn everything of His creation, as far as His gaze reaches."

The meaning of "Light" here is the Light of the Attributes, the vessels that bear the pure meanings. If this Light was unveiled so that the secrets of the Essence were manifested, everything His gaze reached would be annihilated. The truth-realizers consider the intermediary (*wāsiṭa*) to be the very identity of that which it mediates. The disciple continues to pass away from the intermediary by witnessing the Mediated until he totally passes away from the intermediary. Or we might say that he continues to become less aware of the vessels by witnessing the pure meanings until the sun of gnosis rises, whereupon the vessels disappear in the manifestation of the pure meanings, and eye-witnessing occurs when the entities vanish. "God was, and there was nothing with Him; and He is now as He ever was." "What veils you from God is not the presence of a thing that exists alongside Him; what veils you is your delusion that anything exists alongside Him."[356]

In sum, the vision of the Real begins with inner vision, not the eyesight, because inner vision perceives pure meanings, whereas eyesight can only perceive what is physical. But when the inner vision is opened and its Lights overtake the light of the eyesight, the eyesight sees only what the insight sees.[357]

---

356 See the 115th aphorism of al-Iskandarī.
357 *Al-Baḥr al-madīd* vol. 2 p. 391-392.

7.

The Innermost Secret (*al-sirr*)

In the Arabic language:

The word *sirr* means something obscure that is not easily understood, or something a person tries to conceal, whether a word or a deed. The word *sarīra* means something a person keeps secret. [358]

In the Terminology of the Karkariya Order:

The *sirr* is is the subtle reality of divine mercy. This immaculate reality is hallowed beyond the aspirations of servanthood which may deflower it. It is deposited within the kernel of the seed of the heart. The fruit that it yields is the eye-witnessing of the life-breaths of God's exclusive singularity (*aḥadiyya*) that flow through the locus of manifestation of the Essence when it first became determined as a distinct entity.

In the Holy Qur'ān:

The word *sirr* occurs twice in the Holy Qur'ān:

---

358 *Al-Muʻjam al-ʻarabī al-asāsī* p. 619.

God says: **And if thou speakest aloud, verily He knows what is secret and what is more hidden still.** [359]

God says: **Say, "He has sent it down Who knows what is secret in the heavens and on the earth. Truly He is Forgiving, Merciful."** [360]

In the Blessed Hadith:

Abū Hurayra said: "I preserved two stores from God's Messenger ﷺ. As for the first one, I have conveyed it; as for the other, if I were to convey it, this throat of mine would be cut." [361]

'Abd Allāh b. 'Umar ؓ reported that when Ḥafṣa the daughter of 'Umar b. al-Khaṭṭāb became widowed, 'Umar met 'Uthmān b. 'Affān ؓ and suggested that he marry Ḥafṣa. 'Uthmān said he would think it over, and after a few days said he did not feel it was a good time for him to marry. Then 'Umar offered her to Abū Bakr, who gave no reply, which offended 'Umar. Then a few days later God's Messenger ﷺ asked for her hand, and 'Umar accepted. Then 'Umar met Abū Bakr, who said to him, "Perhaps you were angry with me when you offered Ḥafṣa to me and gave no reply." 'Umar replied, "Yes, that is so." He said, "Nothing kept me from replying except that I knew that God's Messenger ﷺ had spoken of her, and I could not divulge the secret of God's Messenger ﷺ. Otherwise, I would have accepted." [362]

---

359 Q Ṭā-Hā 20:7.
360 Q Furqān 25:6.
361 Bukhārī, *Ṣaḥīḥ* #118.
362 Bukhārī, *Ṣaḥīḥ* #3731.

Ibn ʿUmar narrates that God's Messenger ﷺ said, "Do not talk about destiny, for it is God's secret. Do not divulge God's secret." [363]

ʿAbd Allāh b. Masʿūd reported that God's Messenger ﷺ said: "God will gather the first and the last for the appointed meeting for the known Day—standing for forty years, waiting for the matter to be decided between them. God will descend in the shadows of the clouds, from the Throne to the Footstool. And a caller will call out, 'O mankind, would it please you that your Lord, the One who created you, provided for you, and commanded you to worship none but Him and to not associate any partners with Him, should judge that each of you should follow that which he used to follow in the world, and that which he used to worship in the world? Is this not a just ruling from your Lord?' They will respond, 'Certainly.' So they shall proceed forth, and every nation will follow what they used to worship, and the likenesses of their gods they used to worship in the world will appear. Those who used to worship the sun shall proceed forth, as will those who worshiped the moon, those who worshiped stones, and the like. The demonic consort of Jesus will appear with the likeness of Jesus for those who worshiped him, and likewise for the worshippers of ʿUzayr. Then there shall remain Muḥammad ﷺ and his nation. The Lord will present Himself to them and say, 'Why do you not proceed as the people have proceeded?' They will respond, 'We have a Lord

363 *Ḥilyat al-Awliyāʾ* #8396.

whom we have yet to see.' He will say to them, 'If He comes to you, will you recognize Him?' They will respond, 'Between Him and us is a sign; if we see it, we will recognize Him.'[364]

Abū Umāma reported that the Prophet ﷺ said, "The one most pleasing to me is the believer who is penniless but devoted to prayer, who obeys his Lord and worships Him faithfully in secret. He is obscure among the people, no one pays him any mind, and he lives a simple life. His death will come quickly, and few will mourn him, and he will not leave much behind."[365]

✦

As if you see Him (*ka'annaka tarāh*)

It was narrated that Sayyidunā 'Umar b. al Khaṭṭāb said: "We were with God's Messenger ﷺ one day, when there came to us a man wearing dazzling white clothes, with jet black hair. There were no signs of travel on him, and yet none of us knew him. He sat down by the Prophet ﷺ knee to knee, placed his hands on his thighs, and said, 'Muḥammad, tell me about submission (*Islām*). God's Messenger ﷺ replied, 'Submission is to testify that there is no god but God, and that Muḥammad is God's Messenger ﷺ, to perform the prayer, give the alms, fast Ramadan, and perform the pilgrimage to the Holy House if you are able.' He said, 'You have spoken the truth.' We were astonished

---

364 Dāraquṭnī, *Ru'yat Allāh*; see also Bukhārī, *Ṣaḥīḥ* #6913.
365 Aḥmad, *Musnad* #21617.

at how he questioned him and then corroborated him. He then said, 'Tell me about faith (*Īmān*).' He replied, 'It is to believe in God, , His angels, , His books, , His messengers, and the Last Day, and to believe in fate, both the good and the bad.' The man said, 'You have spoken the truth. Now tell me about spiritual excellence (*iḥsān*).' He replied, 'It is to worship God as if you saw Him; for if you see Him not, He assuredly sees you.' He said, 'Tell me about the Hour.' He replied, 'The one questioned knows no more about it than the questioner.' He said, 'Then tell me of its portents.' He replied, 'The slave-girl will give birth to her mistress, and you will see barefoot, naked, needy herdsmen constructing buildings ever higher and higher.' Then the stranger went away, and I tarried a while. Then he said to me: "Umar, do you know who the questioner was?' I replied, 'God and His Messenger know best.' He said, 'It was Jibrīl. He came to you to teach you your religion.'" [366]

When God wanted to be known and to manifest His hidden treasure through itself, He took a handful of His primordial Light and created from it the Throne, the Footstool, the celestial bodies, and the kingdoms. His wisdom dictated that its Lights be covered with the cloak of secrecy and the veil of might, and so the unification of Oneness was manifested in the realm of ephemeral creation. The levels, properties, perspectives, and identities were manifested, while He remained as He ever was: unique, singular, and self-subsisting.

366 Muslim, *Ṣaḥīḥ* #12.

So directions, places, and created beings became distinct, subsisting through the Lights of the divine Attributes, yet effaced by the oneness of the Essence. Hence the holy saying: "I was a hidden treasure, and I loved to be known, so I created creation and acquainted them with Me, and they knew Me."[367]

Thus He became hidden by His Name, manifest by His Essence, and present in everything in the same way as the number one is present in all the numbers. He appeared in oneness through his Name and his Essence, and hid himself in duality through His Name, while remaining in His Essence. Two is nothing more than one plus one, and so on for all the other numbers.

A poet said:

The representation of the cosmos is like Diḥya,[368]
A materialization of the spirit in a deceptive appearance.

Another said:

Nothing remains but God, and no other;
There is no one to arrive, nothing to be distinct.

---

367 Although this ḥadīth is weak in terms of its chain of transmission, it has been mass-transmitted from the great Poles, may God sanctify their secrets, through the path of unveiling.

368 A Companion of the Prophet ﷺ whom he described as resembling the angel Jibrīl.

Thus says the proof of eye-witnessing, for He
Sees nothing but Himself when He looks through my eye.

Someone once said to Junayd ♦, "Do you see your Lord while worshipping Him, or do you believe you can reach Him with your hearts?" Junayd replied, "We would not worship a lord we could not see; nor one whom our eyes saw, lest we compare him to others; nor one unknown to us, lest we be unable to declare his transcendence."

The man asked, "So how do you see Him?"

He replied: "The 'how' is known for mankind, but unknown for the Lord. Eyes will not see Him directly in this world, but hearts may recognize Him through the realities of faith, then ascend from recognition to beholding by witnessing the Light of favor. For He is visible through sacred realities, free from all created attributes, sanctified by His sublime beauty, adorned with His absolute perfection. He graces hearts with His gifts and favors. He is known by his justice, described by His grace."

When he heard this, the man stood up and kissed Junayd's hand and repented, then remained his faithful disciple for the rest of his days, may God have mercy on them both. [369]

So He is veiled through His manifestation, and manifest through His concealment. Eyes fail to see Him only because of the cloak of might and majesty. The created vessels were only made manifest after being covered with the veils of divine clem-

---

369 Ibn ʿAjība, *Īqāẓ al-himam* pp 620-621.

ency and wisdom. Otherwise, they speak in the midst of their stillness and through it, alluding to their Creator, pointing towards their Maker; but no one can understand their glorification. From the *Ḥikam*: "He points to His Names through His traces, and to His Attributes through His Names, and to His Essence through His Attributes; for an attribute cannot exist in and of itself." [370]

Everything exists through Him, manifests through His Essence, issues from His Attributes, nonexistent in His existence, extinguished in His subsistence. The diversity of the phenomena in the universe are but manifestations of the implications of the Names. Flowers may be diverse, but there is only one water.

God says: **Upon the earth are neighboring tracts, vineyards, sown fields, and date palms of a shared root and not of a shared root, watered by one water. And We have favored some above others in bounty. Truly in that are signs for a people who understand.** [371]

God's folk have compared the universe to an ice cube whose external surface is hard while its inside is liquid. The one who looks at the ice cube without any thought would think otherwise, while the one who scrutinizes it carefully would observe that water and ice are identical, and ice is but a manifestation of water. A poet said of this:

---

370 See the 217th aphorism of al-Iskandarī.
371 Q Raʿd 13:4.

The cosmos is like ice,
And you are the water that flows in it.

In reality, ice is but water,
Its property changed by the divine Law;

When it melts, that property changes,
And the property of water reasserts itself.

And in the *Ḥikam*: ""What veils you from God is not the presence of a thing that exists alongside Him; what veils you is your delusion that anything exists alongside Him."[372]

So nothing veils you from God but your illusion that anything other than Him exists, and your regard for the shells of cosmological phenomena. If you took notice of the attributes of Lordship and the might of divinity, you would realize that He is wherever you turn: **To God belong the East and the West. Wheresoever you turn, there is the Face of God. God is All-Encompassing, Knowing.**[373]

Sīdī Ibn ʿAjība ﷺ said:

Know that all places, directions, and created beings subsist through the Lights of the Attributes, and are effaced by the Oneness of the Essence. "God was, and there was nothing with Him; and He is now as He ever was." For nothing possesses existence but God: **Wheresoever you turn, there is the Face of**

---

372 See the 115th aphorism of al-Iskandarī.
373 Q Baqara 2:115.

God. All traces are annihilated by the celestial Lights, and in turn, all Lights are annihilated by the oneness of the secrets, so that none possesses existence but the One.

From the *'Ayniyya*:

My Beloved disclosed Himself in the guises of His beauty,
And in every guise, the Beloved is present.

When His beauty appeared in manifold forms,
They were called by names, each leading to Him.

One of the early Muslims said, "Once I went into a monastery during the time of prayer, and asked a Christian to show me a pure place where I could pray. He replied, 'Purify your heart from everything but Him, and then pray wherever you want.' I was ashamed in front of him."

It is said that Abū Yazīd ﷺ used to pray in any direction he pleased, reciting this verse. According to the people of realization, the "Face of God" means His very Essence, namely the secrets of the Essence and the Lights of the Attributes. He says, **All things perish, save His Face.** [374] That is, everything is annihilated in the past, present, and future, except His hallowed Essence. A poet said of this:

374 Q Qaṣaṣ 28:88.

The gnostics are annihilated, for they no longer witness
Anything but the Sublime Almighty.

They see all else but Him to be perishing,
In the past, the present, and the future.

The knowers of God have passed away from themselves, subsisting through their Lord, and this is why they no longer see anything other than the Real, for they do not believe anything else could exist. A poet said of this:

I have seen no other since I came to know God,
And in truth for us there can be no other.

Ever since I was unified, I have not feared separation,
For today I am united and unified.

To behold anything but the Real nullifies ritual purity, since for the Sufis, to break the bond of annihilation in His attributes by relying on the manifestations of the cosmos is to incur major ritual impurity, for it is the gravest of mortal sins. They performed ablutions with the water of the unseen, which descends from the oceans of the realm of invincibility to the meadows of the spiritual world, and so they became annihilated to their deeds, attributes, and faculties. Then they bathed to wash of their annihilation and shed all that is other-than-Him entirely. They are in constant prayer; ever since they prostrated themselves in the hallowed presence, they have not lifted their heads.

Shaykh Mawlāy Abdul-Salam b. Mashīsh ﷺ said to Abū al-Ḥasan al-Shādhilī ﷺ: "Abū al-Ḥasan, make keen the eye of faith, and you will see God in everything, at everything, with everything, before everything, after everything, above everything, below everything, near everything, and encompassing everything. His nearness is His attribute, and His encompassment is His quality, beyond all extremities and limits, spaces and directions. His company and nearness are not measured in distance, and His encompassment is not a question of encircling His creatures. He erases everything with His Own description: He is the First, the Last, the Manifest, the Hidden. He, is He, is He. God was, and there was nothing with Him; and He is now as He ever was." [375]

If the glory of the God were to manifest in full, the entire universe would come to naught. This is why the divine Acts are the visual manifestations of the Names, the Names the visual manifestations of the Attributes, the Attributes the visual manifestations of the Essence. Thus God is manifest in the midst of His concealment, as His Lights flow through the dense bodies of created things. If He were truly veiled from the world for so much as the blink of an eye, the world would cease to exist.

Sīdī Ibn ʿAjība says in his commentary on the Prayer of Ibn Mashīsh:

---

375 Ibn ʿAjība, *Īqāẓ al-himam* p. 460, 68.

He is Manifest in His concealment, Hidden in His manifestations. His Name the Manifest (*al-Ẓāhir*) erases the manifestation of other-than-Him and conceals it, for there can be no other manifest but Him. His Name the Hidden (*al-Bāṭin*) necessitates the manifestation of His self-disclosures, so that He may be hidden relative to their outward senses. If He remained ever hidden, He would not be known or worshipped. Thus He alone is the Manifest and the Hidden; anything that manifests is He, and anything that is hidden is He.

Or you might say that He is the outward manifestation of all that is hidden, and the hidden secret of all that manifests, which is all divine, since there is nothing besides Him.

Or you might say that He is the Manifest in regard to bestowal of knowledge, and the Hidden in regard to modality, since the divine Essence is beyond modality.

Or you might say that He is Manifest through His wisdom, and Hidden through His omnipotence, which is the cause of His wisdom; for He manifested wisdom, but concealed omnipotence. [376]

It has been said:

Nothing remains but the Real, and no other;
Hence, there is no one to arrive, and nothing to be distinct.

376 Ibn 'Ajība, *Sharḥ ṣalāt al-Quṭb Ibn Mashīsh*, p. 51.

The proof for this comes by way of eye-witnessing, for He
Sees nothing but Himself when He looks through my eye.

It has also been said:

All mortals are but a manifestation-sites of My guise,
They subsist through the resplendent beauty of My Face.

I manifest through the attributes of all creatures,
Indeed! My dazzling Light discloses in all the essences.

✣

The Vicegerency (*al-khilāfa*)

God says: **And when thy Lord said to the angels, "I am placing a vicegerent upon the earth," they said, "Wilt Thou place therein one who will work corruption therein, and shed blood, while we hymn Thy praise and call Thee Holy?" He said, "Truly I know what you know not."** [377]

When the Real wanted to be known, He created the Adam of existence in His own image, clothed him with His attributes, breathed the spirit of His secrets into him, and made him the mirror of His perfections and the locus of His beauty.

377 Q Baqara 2:30.

Abū Hurayra reported that the Prophet ﷺ said, "God created Adam in His image, sixty cubits tall. When He created him, He said 'Go and greet those angels sitting over there, and listen to how they reply to you, for that will be your greeting and the greeting of your progeny.' So Adam said, 'Peace be upon you', and they replied, 'And upon you be peace and God's mercy', adding 'and God's mercy.' All those who enter Paradise will have the image of Adam. Ever since then, mankind has been diminishing in size." [378]

Ibn 'Umar reported that God's Messenger ﷺ said, "Do not vilify the face, for the son of Adam was created in the image of the All-Merciful." [379]

This creature thus has a sublime rank and a pure origin, having been shaped in the best possible stature; for he is the presence of unification. All that was dispersed through the cosmos is folded up within him, and all that was separated is unified in him. All created beings are subordinate to Him, and not he to them. They serve and defend him, for he bears of the secret of lordly expansion in his heart. The divine establishment (*al-istiwā' al-ilāhī*) over the human heart differs from the establishment of the All-Merciful over the luminous Throne. For the divine establishment is at the center of the circle, whereas the All-Merciful's establishment is its circumference.

378 Bukhārī, *Ṣaḥīḥ* #5788.
379 Ibn Abī 'Āṣim, *Sunna* #416.

As such, man is the original seed, whereas the universe and all that it contains is the tree that sprouts from it. The world is the image, and man is its spirit. To this effect, a poet once said:

O precursor in the procession of creation,
And successor in the ranks of invention,

Understand that you are the blueprint of existence,
And no being is greater in God's sight than you.

Are the Throne and the Footstool not within you,
And the higher and lower worlds?

The whole cosmos is but a great man.
And you are a microcosm like it.

Making a parallel with grammar, we can say that the original status of the human being in the sentence of existence is that he is the powerless object of the verb on which the property of the verb acts by the will of the subject. However, the wisdom of concealment phrased the sentence in the passive voice, so that the human being became the implicit subject, the delegate of the actual subject, when before he was the object, and thus he was raised (*marfū'*) after having been burdened (*manṣūb*) and degraded. [380] Therefore it was only fitting that the angels pros-

---

380 *Marfū'*, literally "raised", is the grammatical designation of the subject in Arabic, while *manṣūb*, literally "burdened", is that of the object.

trate to him, for he is the vicegerent and delegate of the presence of the Real concealed in him.

His intellect is the manifestation of knowledge, his image the manifestation of will, his aspiration the manifestation of power, and his imagination the manifestation of being. Thus, the human kingdom is the meeting-place of the lordly realities and their forms; and this is why I told you earlier, "Do not come out of your grave."

The hadith of the *walī* contains a tremendous allusion for those whose minds God has expanded. The Beloved ﷺ tells us that his Almighty Lord says, "Whosoever shows enmity to a friend (*walī*) of Mine, I declare war on them. My servant does not draw near to Me with anything more loved to Me than that which I made obligatory upon him; and My servant continues to draw near to me with supererogatory devotions until I love him. When I love him, I am his hearing with which he hears, and his sight with which he sees, and his hand with which he strikes, and his foot with which he walks. Were he to ask something of Me, I would surely give it to him; and were he to seek refuge with Me, I would surely grant him refuge. I do not hesitate about anything so much as I hesitate about seizing the soul of My faithful servant: he hates death, and I hate to displease him." [381]

Look with the eye of your heart at this beautiful allusion, which has confounded the minds of those who seek to uphold

---

381 Bukhārī, *Ṣaḥīḥ* #6050.

God's transcendence in such a cold and obtuse way, which neither God nor His Blessed Messenger ﷺ ever commanded us to do.

The secret of all things is thus found within their opposites; and the Real can only be known by unifying opposites. The imperfections of servanthood are, in reality, nothing other than the secret manifestations of the perfections of Lordship.

In the *Ḥikam*: "The cosmos can contain you only with regard to your body; it cannot contain you with regard to your spirit." [382]

Sīdī Ibn 'Ajība explains this aphorism as follows:

When the spirit is purified from all the turbidities of the sensory realm, it ascends to the realm of invincibility, and then nothing can veil it from God, whether the earth, the heavens, the cosmos, the Throne, or the Footstool, for all of them become insignificant to it. This is something that the gnostics experience; when they observe the universe, they see it melting and returning to the state of water. And when they drink this water, it becomes in their hearts like a single drop. However, their capacity to encompass the universe differs from one to the other: for some, the drop is the size of an egg, while for others it is the size of a mustard seed. This depends on the scope of their vision and whether it is broad or narrow. Each time the spirit swims in the ocean of invincibility, the universe is contracted for it [i.e. the spirit] so that it is no longer aware of it.

---

382 See the 25th aphorism of al-Iskandarī.

This is why one of them said, "If the Throne was in the corner of the gnostic's heart, he would not realize it." Another said, "The Throne and the Footstool are but engravings upon my shield."

The shaykh of our shaykhs, Mawlāy ʿAbd al-Qādir al-Jīlānī ﷺ (d. 1166), said, "The Throne and the Footstool are folded up in my grasp."

The universe then comes to naught and dissolves, and the spiritual world connects with the world of invincibility, so that nothing remains but the Living One who never dies. This is something that only the gnostics can understand, those whose spiritual sides dominate their human to the point that they are beings of pure spirit, their bodies residing with other people while their spirits reside with God.

O human being! The universe can contain your physical human nature and your limited form, but it cannot contain your spirit, because your spirit is connected to the all-encompassing world of invincibility. But since it has become dense and is restricted in this physical frame, the spirit is veiled by the divine wisdom and restricted by the divine omnipotence. So long as the lower human nature remains dense because of love for base desires and habits, it will remain veiled. But when it becomes subtle and airy through remembrance of God, and the sensory veil is burned away from it, it will return to its origin and connect with its ocean. The spiritual and physical worlds then yield to its grasp, and neither the earth nor the heavens can contain it. This is why it is said that the earth cannot hold the Sufi, nor can the sky remain above him. [383]

In this sense, Sayyidunā Ibn ʿArabī wrote the following verses:

When she kills with her gaze, her speech restores to life,
As though she, in giving life thereby, were Jesus.

Her Torah is the tablet of her legs in splendor;
I recite and study it as though I were Moses.

A priestess, a daughter of Rome, unadorned:
You see her human form bathed in radiance.

Wild is she, none can make her his friend;
In her chamber she has made a tomb of remembrance.

She has baffled everyone who is learned in our religion,
And every cleric, every rabbi, every priest.

---

383   Ibn ʿAjība, *Īqāẓ al-himam* pp 520-521.

Conclusion

Ibn Mas'ūd narrated that God's Messenger ﷺ recited, **Whomsoever God wishes to guide, He expands his breast for submission,** [384] then he ﷺ said, "When the Light enters the heart, it expands." Someone said, "O Messenger of God, is there a sign to show this?" He answered, "Yes: aversion to the illusory abode, longing for the eternal abode, and preparation for death before it comes." [385]

When God wishes to favor one of His servants and bring him closer, He guides him to the companionship of someone who will plant in his heart a seed of Muḥammadan Light, then water it with litanies and spiritual replenishment, until the tree of divine contentment grows in him; **its roots firmly fixed** in the earth of his heart **and its branches** rising high into **the heaven** of secrets, **bringing forth fruit in every season.** [386] At that moment, his breast becomes expanded in order to receive the Light of divine disclosure. The breezes of yearning and love blow through his heart, and the veil is lifted to reveal the ascending route of divine beauty. It is then that he leaves all that

384 Q An'ām 6:125.
385 Ḥākim, *Mustadrak* #7948.
386 Q Ibrāhīm 14:24-25.

he loves and forsakes the comfort of this illusory abode, his spirit longing for its Creator.

Stand-up, then, and act without further delay, for God says: **When thou art free, exert thyself; and let thy desire be for thy Lord.** [387] Procrastination is one of the Devils' greatest allies, and death does not ask permission when it comes: **We seized them suddenly, while they were unaware.** [388]

Leave everything that obstructs your Path, cut the bonds that veil you from the divine presence, and stop following the caprices of your lower self. The Beloved ﷺ said, "The wise man is the one who calls himself to account, and works for what will come after death; and the foolish man is the one who indulges his soul in its caprice, and then expects God to reward him." [389]

God has granted you countless blessings, and on top of that, you are in good health. The Prophet ﷺ said, "There are two blessings of which a great many people cheat themselves: health, and free time." [390]

If you are seeking a remedy for your illness, come to us. If you wish to know God, stop reading other people's books—**read your book**, and discover who you are. Do not skip a single line, until you behold the secret of your vicegerency, and know your Lord through your Lord. **Read your book! On this Day, your soul suffices as a reckoner against you.** [391]

387 Q Sharḥ 94:6-7.
388 Q Aʿrāf 7:95.
389 Ibn Mājah, *Sunan* 4258.
390 Bukhārī, *Ṣaḥīḥ* #5962.
391 Q Isrāʾ 17:14.

The Sufi must always be in a state of meditation, remembrance, or contemplation. Come to us so that you may gather the three into one, and taste the proximity of the One who is incomparable. Learn what true love is, and rectify your relationship to your own soul, until the wolf of your non-existence grazes in the company of the sheep of your existence; until the fire of your passion mixes with the water of your spirit; until you exit your shell, which is bound by the six directions, and heal your short-sighted vision, which is limited to the phenomena of temporality; until you escape the confines of space and time, and enter the presence of the Real.

God chose you among all His creatures, and spoke to none other than you! He penned you with the ink of the spirit upon the page of existence. So **read in the Name of your Lord**, the book of yourself, and you will recognize the Real in all things.

Works Cited

1. Abū Dawūd al-Sijistānī, Sulaymān b. al-Asha‘th. *Sunan Abī Dawūd*. Beirut: Dār al-Kutub al-‘Ilmīya, 2019.

2. Abū Nu‘aym al-Iṣfahāni, Aḥmad b. ‘Abd Allāh. *Ḥilyat al-awlīyā’ wa-ṭabaqāt al-aṣfiyā’*. Egypt: al-Sa‘āda, 1996.

3. al-‘Alawī, Aḥmad. *al-Minaḥ al-quddūsīya fī Sharḥ al-Murshid al-mu‘īn bi-ṭarīq al-ṣūfīya*. Beirut: Dār Ibn Zaydūn, 1987.

4. al-Albānī, Muḥammad Nāṣir al-Dīn. *Silsilat al-aḥādīth al-ḍa‘īfa wa’l-mawḍu‘a*. Riyadh: Maktabat al-Ma‘ārif, 1992.

5. al-Baghawī, Abū Muḥammad al-Ḥusayn. *Mu‘jam al-ṣaḥāba*. Kuwait: Dār al-Bayān, 2000.

6. al-Baqlī, Abū Muḥammad Rūzbihān. *Tafsīr ‘Arā’is al-bayān fī ḥaqā’iq al-Qur’ān*. Beirut: Dār al-Kutub al-‘Ilmīya, 2008.

7. al-Bayhaqī, Aḥmad b. al-Ḥusayn. *Dalā’il al-nubuwwa wa-ma‘rifat aḥwāl ṣāḥib al-sharī‘a*. Beirut: Dār al-Kutub al-‘Ilmīya, 2020.

8. —*Shu‘ab al-Imān*. Riyadh: Maktabat al-Rushd, 2003.

9. al-Bazzār, Abū Bakr Aḥmad. *al-Baḥr al-zakhkhār*. Beirut: Mu’assasat ‘Ulūm al-Qur’ān, 1988.

10. al-Bukhārī, Muḥammad b. Ismā‘īl. *Ṣaḥīḥ al-Bukhārī*. Beirut: Dār Iḥyā’ al-Turāth al-‘Arabīya, 1981.

11. al-Darqāwī, Mūlāy al-‘Arabī. *Rasā’il Mūlāy al-‘Arabī al-Darqāwī al-musammat Bushūr al-hadīya fī madhhab al-ṣūfiya*. Beirut: Dār al-Kutub al-‘Ilmīya, 2009.

12. al-Dāraquṭnī, Abū al-Ḥasan ʿAlī b. ʿUmar. *Ru'yat Allāh*. Zarqa, Jordan: Maktabat al-Manār, 1990/1.

13. al-Ghazālī, Abū Ḥāmid Muḥammad. *Iḥyā' 'ulūm al-dīn*. Beirut: Dār al-Maʿrifa, 1982.

14. al-Ḥaffār, Hilāl b. Muḥammad. *Juz' Hilāl al-Ḥaffār*. Riyadh: Dār al-Atharīya, 2007.

15. al-Ḥākim al-Naysābūrī, Muhammad b. ʿAbd Allāh. *al-Mustadrak ʿalā al-ṣaḥīḥayn fī al-ḥadīth*. Beirut: Dār al-Kutub al-ʿIlmīya, 1990.

16. al-Hunā'ī, ʿAlī b. al-Ḥasan. *al-Munjid fī al-lugha wa'l-aʿlām*. Cairo: ʿĀlam al-Kutub, 1988.

17. Ibn Abī ʿĀṣim, Abū Bakr. *Sunna*. Beirut: Maktabat al-Islāmī, 2010.

18. Ibn Abī Shayba, ʿAbd Allāh. *al-Muṣannaf*. Riyadh: Maktabat al-Rushd, 2004.

19. Ibn ʿAjība, Aḥmad. *Tafsīr al-Baḥr al-madīd fī tafsīr al-Qur'ān al-majīd*. Beirut: Dār al-Kutub al-ʿIlmīya, 2002.

20. —*Futūḥāt al-ilāhīya fī sharḥ al-Mabāḥith al-aṣlīya*. Beirut: Dār al-Kutub al-ʿIlmīya, 2010.

21. —*Īqāẓ al-himam fī sharḥ al-Ḥikam*. Beirut: Dār al-Kutub al-ʿIlmīya, 2016.

22. —*Kitāb Sharḥ Ṣalāt al-quṭb Ibn Mashīsh*. Casablanca: Dār al-Rashād al-Ḥadītha, ND.

23. Ibn al-ʿAsākir, ʿAlī b. al-Ḥasan. *Tarīkh Dimashq*. Beirut: Dār al-Kutub al-ʿIlmīya, 2012

24. Ibn ʿAshir, ʿAbd al-Wāḥid, *Al-Murshid al-Mu'een: The Concise Guide to the Basics of the Deen*. Translated by Asadullah Yate. Bradford, UK: The Diwan Press, 2013.

25. Ibn ʿAṭāʾ Allāh al-Iskandarī. *al-Qaṣd al-mujarrad fī maʿri-fat al-ism al-mufrad wa-yalīhī Ḥabbat al-maḥabba*. Beirut: Dār al-Kutub al-ʿIlmīya, 2013.

26. —*The Pure Intention: On Knowledge of the Unique Name*. Translated by Khalid Williams. Cambridge, England: Islamic Texts Society, 2018.

27. —*al-Ḥikam al-ʿaṭāʾiya al-kubrā waʾl-ṣughrā waʾl-munājāt al-il-āhīya waʾl-mukātabāt*. Beirut: Dār al-Kutub al-ʿIlmīya, 2017.

28. —*Ibn ʿAtaʾillah: The Book of Wisdom/ Kwaja Abdullah Ansari: Intimate Conversations*. Introduction, Translation, and Notes of the Book of Wisdom by Victor Danner and of Intimate Conversations by Wheeler M. Thackston. New York: Paulist Press, 1978.

29. Ibn Ḥajar al-Haytamī, Shihāb al-Dīn. *Fatḥ al-ilāh fī sharḥ al-mishkāt*. Beirut: Dār al-Kutub al-ʿIlmīya, 2015.

30. Ibn Ḥajar al-ʿAsqalānī, Shihāb al-Dīn, *Fatḥ al-Bārī bi-sharḥ Ṣaḥīḥ al-Bukhārī*. Cairo: al-Maktaba al-Salafīya, ND.

31. Ibn Ḥanbal, Aḥmad. *Musnad*. Qatar: Wizārat al-Awqāf waʾl-Shuʾūn al-Islāmīya, ND.

32. al-Haythamī, ʿAlī b. Abī Bakr b. Sulaymān. *Kashf al-astār ʿan zawāʾid al-Bazz*ār. Beirut: Muʾassasat al-Risāla, 1979.

33. Ibn Ḥibbān, Muḥammad. *Ṣaḥīḥ Ibn Ḥibbān*. Beirut: Muʾassasat al-Risāla, 1993.

34. Ibn Kathīr, Abū al-Fidāʾ Ismāʿīl b. ʿUmar. *Tafsīr al-Qurʾān al-ʿaẓīm*. Beirut: Dār Ibn Ḥazm, 1996.

35. Ibn Mājah, ʿAbd Allāh Muḥammad Yazīd al-Qazwīnī. *Sunan*. Beirut: Dār Iḥyāʾ al-Kutub al-ʿArabīya, ND.

36. al-Qayyim al-Jawzīya, Muḥammad b. Abī Bakr. *Madārij al-Sālikīn*. Beirut: Dār al-Kitāb al-ʿArabī, 2003.

37. Ibn Rajab al-Ḥanbalī, Zayn al-Dīn. *Jāmiʿ al-ʿulūm wa'l-ḥikam fī sharḥ khamsīn ḥadīthan min jawāmiʿ al-kalim*. Beirut: Dār Ibn Ḥazm, 2017.

38. Ibn Taymīyya, Taqī al-Dīn. *Majmūʿ al-fatāwī Shaykh al-Islām Aḥmad Ibn Taymīyya*. Beirut: Dār al-Kutub al-ʿIlmīya, 2011.

39. ʿIyād b. Mūsā. *al-Shifā bi-taʿrīf ḥuqūq al-Muṣṭafā*. Beirut: Dār al-Kutub al-ʿIlmīya, 2019.

40. al-Jīlī, ʿAbd al-Karīm. *al-Insān al-kāmil fī maʿrifat al-awākhir wa'l-awwā'il*. Beirut: Dār al-Kutub al-ʿIlmīya, 2016.

41. al-Kasanzān, Muḥammad. *Mawsūʿat al-Kasanzānī fīmā iṣṭalaḥa ʿalayhi ahl al-taṣawwuf wa'l-ʿirfān*. Beirut: Dār Āya, ND.

42. Ibn Khallikān, Abū al-ʿAbbās Aḥmad, *Wafayāt al-aʿyān wa-ānbā' abnā' al-zamān*. Beirut: Dār Ṣadir, 1972.

43. al-Maqdisī, ʿAbd al-Ghanī. *al-Kamāl fī asmā' al-rijāl*. Kuwait: al-Hay'at al-ʿĀma li'l-ʿInāya bi'l-Ṭibāʿa wa-nashr al-Qur'ān al-Karīm wa'l-Sunna al-Nabawīya wa-ʿUlūmihā, 2016.

44. *al-Muʿjam al-ʿArabī al-asāsī: li'l-Nāṭiqīn bi'l-ʿarabīya wa mutʿalimīhā*. Paris: Librairie Larousse. ND.

45. Muslim, Abū al-Ḥusayn b. al-Ḥajjāj al-Naysabūrī. *Ṣaḥīḥ Muslim*. Beirut: Dār Iḥyā' al-Kutub al-ʿArabīya, ND.

46. Nasr, Seyyed Hossein et al. *The Study Quran: a new translation and commentary*. New York, NY: HarperOne, an imprint of HarperCollins Publishers, 2017.

47. al-Nawawī, Yaḥyā b. Sharaf. *Sharḥ al-Arbaʿīn al-nawawīya fī al-aḥādith al-ṣaḥīḥa al-nabawīya.* Damascus: Maktabat Dār al-Fatḥ, 1984.

48. al-Qushayrī, ʿAbd al-Karīm. *Laṭāʾif al-ishārāt tafsīr Qushayrī.* Cairo: al-Hayʾa al-Miṣrīya al-ʿĀma, 2000.

49. al-Rifāʿī, Aḥmad. *al-Burhān al-Muʾayyad.* Egypt: Maṭbaʿat al-Ẓāhir, ND.

50. al-Shawkānī, Muḥammad b.ʿAlī. *Qaṭr al-Walī ʿalā ḥadīth al-walī.* Beirut: Dār al-Kutub al-ʿIlmīya, 2001.

51. al-Shushtarī, Abū ʿAlī b. ʿAbd Allāh, and Saʿd ibn Aḥmad Ibn Luyūn al-Tujībī. *al-Risālah al-Shushtarīyah, aw al-Risāla al-ʿilmīyah fī al-taṣawwuf: Talkhīṣ al-Ināla aľilmīya.* Edited by Muḥammad al-ʿAdlūnī Idrīsī. Casablanca: Dār al-Thaqāfah, 2004.

52. al-Suyūṭī, Jalāl al-Dīn. *al-Ḥāwī liʾl-fatāwī.* Beirut: Dār al-Kutub al-ʿIlmīya, 2000.

53. —*al-Ḥāwī liʾl-fatāwī.* Beirut: Dār al-Kutub al-ʿIlmīya, 2000.

54. al-Ṭabarānī, Sulaymān b. Aḥmad. *al-Muʿjam al-kabīr.* Beirut, Riyadh: Maktabat al-Maʿārif, ND. *al-Muʿjam al-awsaṭ.* Riyadh: Maktabat al-Maʿārif, ND.

55. al-Ṭabarī, Abū al-Qāsim Hibat Allāh b. al-Ḥasan. *Karāmāt al-Awliyāʾ.* Riyadh: Dār al-Ṭayba, 1992.

56. al-Tirmidhī, Muḥammad b. ʿĪsā. *al-Jāmiʿ al-ṣaḥīḥ sunan al-Tirmidhī.* Beirut: Dār Iḥyāʾ al-Turāth al-ʿArabīya, ND.

57. al-Tujībī, Ibn Luyūn. *al-Ināla al-ʿilmīya.* Casablanca: Dār al-Thaqāfa, 2004.

Printed and bound
in the United States of America